From North Africa
to the Arakan

From North Africa to the Arakan

The Engrossing Memoir of a WWII Spitfire Ace

Alan McGregor Peart DFC

GRUB STREET · LONDON

Published by
Grub Street
4 Rainham Close
London
SW11 6SS

British Library Cataloguing in Publication Data
Peart, Alan McGregor
   From North Africa to the Arakan: the engrossing memoir
   of WWII Spitfire ace Alan McGregor Peart, DFC
   1. Peart, Alan McGregor 2. Fighter pilots – New Zealand
   3. World War, 1939-1945 – Aerial operations, British
   4. World War, 1939-1945 – Pesonnel narratives, New Zealand
   I. Title
   940.5'44'941'092

ISBN 13: 978 1 906502 03 4

Cover design by Lizzie B Design

Formatted by Pearl Graphics, Hemel Hempstead

Printed and bound by MPG Ltd, Bodmin, Cornwall

Grub Street only uses FSC
(Forest Stewardship Council) paper for its books.

Contents

Dedication

This book is dedicated to the memory of my comrades and colleagues-in-arms of 610 and 81 Squadrons, RAF, many of whom gave their lives and have no known graves. They came from near and far to defend their lands against the onslaught of a dangerous foe. And to the ground crews who supported their pilots at the cost of extreme fatigue, bad living conditions, and the risk of enemy attack.

The debt we owe is great, and to them much honour is due.

Acknowledgements

My memoirs were written primarily for the attention and possible interest of later generations of my family. However, I wish to acknowledge the contribution of Larry Hill, Auckland, but for whose gentle persuasion this book would not have been published. Larry has used his expertise with the computer in the setting out and general shaping of the content material to a degree which I could never have achieved. Thank you Larry.

I also wish to thank Larry Cronin Jnr, the son of my closest 81 Squadron comrade and friend Larry Cronin Snr, with whom I have been in close contact for many years since the death of his father. Larry Jnr has also assisted me in the preparation of this book in many ways including his encouragement and support. Thank you Larry Jnr.

Finally I thank my wife Jennifer, without whose advice and help I would have trod into forbidden territory, my daughter Judith and sons Robert and Alastair for their interest and encouragement, and my daughter-in-law Caroline for her many hours of typing.

Thank you all!

Alan McGregor Peart

Foreword

From 1942 until 1944 Alan Peart and my father Laurance Cronin (known as Larry) flew Spitfires on operational duties with 81 RAF Fighter Squadron over Gibraltar, North Africa, Malta, Sicily, Italy, India and Burma. Both were extremely lucky to survive the flying war as the majority of 81's original pilots and pilot replacements did not. After the war both Alan and my father kept in touch and remained firm friends until my father's passing in 1991 aged 72 years.

My father often spoke to me of his hair-raising wartime flying experiences with 81 Squadron, and in particular, about his close friend and fellow pilot Alan Peart. They had been together through many exhausting air battles fighting both the Germans and Japanese who were usually excellent and skilled pilots in their own right.

Toward the end of the war at age twenty-two Alan returned home to New Zealand. On reaching home he was physically ill, totally worn out and extremely stressed subsequent to his years of daily operational flying against the enemy. Because of his health problems and after a furlough with the war still on, Alan was transferred to the New Zealand Central Flying School to become a flying instructor on Harvard aircraft. This took him out of operational flying. After the war it took Alan several years fully to recover from the stress of his operational flying years. In 1945 Alan resumed his civilian life and a successful career.

It was not until 1974 that my father and Alan caught up with one another again when my parents travelled from Australia to New Zealand. My mother later said it was a most moving reunion as both men greeted one another again for the first time in thirty years. They hugged and tears flowed. Their flying days had come back to them. Their few days together were spent reliving past times as they reviewed their flying logbooks and photo albums and remembered their many lost fellow pilots of 81 RAF Squadron who had not returned home thirty years earlier.

My father had the utmost admiration and respect for his friend Alan Peart, both as a person and as a skilled fighter pilot. Alan had spent many hours flying Hurricanes before Spitfires and had run up quite a score making him an ace. Amongst many things I recall, my father once noted that Alan was a 'tough boy' who took the enemy's destruction very seriously. He said Alan had replaced the fire axe mounted in the cockpit of his Spitfire with a Sten gun and spare magazines for use against the enemy in the event of being shot down behind the lines. Even on the ground Alan didn't intend to go down without a good fight! A tribute to Alan Peart is recorded in *Aces High* published by Grub Street.

Through my much missed late father, it is my great privilege personally to know Spitfire fighter ace Alan McGregor Peart DFC. I firmly recommend this book to anyone interested in a gripping true account of a young man's private air battle to defend the Empire, who, with great flying skill and God's guiding hand, managed to survive the war.

Larry Cronin (Jnr)
Alexandra 3714
Australia

1
Salerno

History records the invasion of Salerno by the Allied forces, in September 1943, as a near disaster. The bridgehead, containing an airstrip for supply purposes, was put under severe pressure by the Germans, who very nearly overran it. We were required to fly with long-range tanks over the sea past Stromboli (a volcano called the lighthouse of the Mediterranean) to the Salerno bridgehead where we had time for a half-hour patrol. There were Seafires stationed on the airstrip, and American fighters were patrolling high above, so it seemed that enemy aircraft would have a hard time penetrating such an umbrella. The airstrip was in full use all day with supply C47s landing one behind another. No air control of any type existed. I was in a flight of six Spitfires over Salerno when we saw a battleship in Salerno Bay suddenly explode. This turned out to be HMS *Warspite*.

We had entered the busy arena at Angels 10 (10,000 feet), well under the umbrella of American P38s (twin-engined Lightnings) at about Angels 20. The place buzzed with British and American C47s (Dakotas) bringing in supplies, and every now and again one or more of the P38s would dive down seemingly to attack other friendly aircraft (there were no enemy planes that we could see) which happened to be flying over the beachhead. We hoped that the aircraft recognition of the Americans, though reputedly poor, was good enough to keep them away from us, but we did expect that they would have picked up any German bombers so daring as to enter the area unescorted in broad daylight. Our patrol had just started with the expectation that things would remain normal and quiet, as far as the air was concerned anyway. How wrong we were!

When the warship in the bay suddenly erupted in flames I immediately assumed that a submarine must have torpedoed it, however the sea was calm with no sign of the telltale foam trails of torpedoes, so I scanned the space around us more closely. I was astounded to see three Dornier bombers racing away to the north. It was their bombs which had hit the warship, and they turned out to be the first radio-guided bombs used in the war. Although the air was thick with allied fighters, these three aircraft had crept in quite unnoticed. How on earth had we missed them? It was very hazy, and while we always kept a good lookout for enemy aircraft within our three-mile visual range, those we encountered were nearly always fighters above us. Bombers we hardly ever saw. Why hadn't the Americans seen them?

With no hesitation we opened our throttles wide and took off after them. The three bombers had split up to make things difficult and Bill Goby, with his number two chased one bomber whilst I with my number two, Bryan Young, and Bill Fell with his number two all found ourselves chasing another. The third escaped our attention, fortunately for him. We were soon in an attacking position with my two out to one side at a slightly higher altitude, and Fell's pair overtaking the rear of the Dornier at high speed. The bomber crew showed all the signs of hardened experience by weaving around as we approached and suddenly changing position as we came within firing range. The defending gunners were very accurate.

Bill Fell precipitately made the first attack from directly astern aiming to get in a telling burst. The enemy gunner promptly hit him hard in reply. Fortunately for Bill the big Rolls-Royce Merlin engine in front took the brunt of the fire and he wasn't killed or wounded. However he took no further part in the action. His number two pulled away to join us. I attacked next from an angle on the port side deliberately applying slipping and skidding as I approached. As I came within range I straightened up, applied deflection in front of the target, and opened fire with both cannons and machine guns.

The defending gunners fired back and the bomber weaved in defence. Nothing happened for about a second and then flashes of bursting cannon shells appeared on the bomber's port wing. I broke off to one side making sure that I was slipping in one direction while appearing to be flying in another. This made it difficult for the opposing gunner to shoot accurately. I saw one of the gunners as I disengaged from close in but he wasn't watching me. He seemed more interested in the others preparing for their attack I supposed. Nevertheless

I could not risk an assumption which might be wrong.

My two colleagues also made attacks, without apparent result. I then made my second attack adopting the same approach tactics while the bomber pilot did his best to dodge. I opened fire again with both cannons and machine guns, and this time my fire hit the bomber solidly. A large piece flew off and there was a big bang as my aeroplane flew into it. I broke off my attack and checked all instruments to see if anything was badly amiss. Meanwhile the other two each had a further go but again seemingly without result.

The Dornier 217, for that is what it turned out to be, was losing height and it eventually crash landed on the side of a scrub-covered hill. While obviously badly damaged it was not on fire, and I thought that at least some of the crew might have survived. The other two Spitfire pilots were keen to strafe the downed aircraft as it had crashed in enemy territory and the crew could possibly have been rescued to fight again. On the other hand the bravery of the crew in carrying out an operation unescorted by fighters in the face of overwhelming odds was most impressive. They had defended themselves with great determination and skill. They deserved the chance to live so I ordered the other two off. We never did find out whether there were any survivors.

Unfortunately, that was far from the end of the mission for us. Much more painful scenes were to follow. Indeed a little good fortune might have prevented at least some of them. To begin with we became aware that Bill Fell's aircraft, which had been badly hit in his first attack, was on fire and calling for assistance. We quickly picked him up by his smoke trail some distance away and flew to his aid. Obviously he had to leave his aircraft at the earliest possible moment. In his favour he had sufficient height to use his parachute but was having difficulty in controlling his Spitfire. We gave him the standard procedure for abandoning his aircraft, and he did his best to carry this out while we could do no more than watch with some trepidation.

His aeroplane was trailing smoke and flame and things in his cockpit must have been decidedly uncomfortable. The abandon aircraft procedure required him to trim his aeroplane heavily nose down ready for rolling it upside down. Having done this he had to hold the aircraft level against a strong tendency to dive. He had next to undo the electrical connections to his helmet, unclip an oxygen tube, jettison his plastic canopy, release his Sutton harness which normally held him tightly to his seat, roll the aircraft upside down, and eject himself downwards so that he would miss the tail. When entirely clear of the aeroplane he would pull the D ring near his waist and release his parachute. This sounds nicely sequential but when the temperature in the cockpit is searing and things are burning and it can be expected that the sequence can become a little hurried, even essential bits can be overlooked. The imminent probability of an almighty explosion could also spur a too rapid execution of the exit procedures. Bill had all of these problems to face.

Fell rolled his Spitfire onto its back and left the cockpit, but as so often happens, things did not go to plan. The aeroplane immediately started to dive before he was clear, and his parachute deployed at the same time. Some other pilots who had successfully used the same procedure in the past, had told us that they pushed the control column hard forward with their feet as they exited the cockpit. This would have stopped the rapid dive which happened in Bill Fell's case. Anyway Fell's parachute hooked over the tail plane and the machine, with Fell trailing behind, dived vertically to the ground. We watched in horror at the certain loss of a well liked and experienced colleague.

However, just before reaching the ground he broke free and to our surprise his parachute opened. The aeroplane went in with an explosion and a great gout of flame and smoke, while Bill did one swing in his harness before his body disappeared through trees to hit the ground close by. My conclusion was that in the circumstances he would have escaped with his life, but possibly with broken limbs. My two colleagues didn't see the parachute open and reported Bill's certain demise to the squadon intelligence officer upon their return. Who was right? Three or four days later Fell turned up at our squadron uninjured, having been captured by the enemy, and having escaped back through our lines. I think he survived the war too.

Now we were faced with a shortage of fuel and having to land at the one airstrip within the Salerno beachhead. We headed in the direction of a great mushroom of dust which indicated the location of the heavily used strip. As we neared it I told my two colleagues that each was on his own and to land as quickly as possible. Landing safely was quite a tall order as there was a queue of Dakotas in the circuit all trying to put down into a thick pall of dust which completely obscured the strip itself. Anti-aircraft guns located at various points around the perimeter were firing at some unknown target, very likely the American Lightnings patrolling above. We could see no other purpose! I was becoming very concerned that my machine might not last much longer as it had been damaged in the engagement and my instruments told me that something was seriously wrong. I made one attempt to get into the circuit but was cut off by a Dakota forcing its way just in front of me.

In desperation I flew over the top of another one following and gave him my slipstream. He wobbled badly and gave way so I entered the dust pall on my landing approach. Visibility was minimal (only a few yards it seemed) but I managed to put my Spitfire down somewhere at the start of the strip with the hope that everything was clear in front. To my horror while still at speed another Spitfire loomed up sitting on the strip right in front of me. I had no recourse but to veer off the strip into the rough on the left hand side. There my aeroplane hit some obstacle and went onto its nose into a vertical position. My first reaction was one of anger at the stupid fool who had forced me to lose the first machine in my flying career. Then I became alarmed at the thought that my machine may go right over onto its back, possibly trapping me in the cockpit. But I was lucky because it chose to fall back onto its undercarriage.

I felt furious and quitted the cockpit in a hurry to go to the stalled machine on the strip. I have no idea how he came to be there but he was Goby's number two. Other machines were rushing past invisibly in the dust and every now and again there was the sound of a destructive collision. It was essential that we got clear of the runway as quickly as possible. Together we managed to move the Spitfire which weighed approximately three tons, over a little way from which position the pilot could safely start the engine and taxi out of trouble. I went back to my aeroplane and decided reluctantly that it had to be abandoned. Anti-aircraft fire was still going on and explosions indicating that shellfire seemed to be occurring in the vicinity. I thought that I heard the odd plucking sound which suggested machine gun bullets passing by.

The strip area was indeed being shelled and I decided that I had better find some cover. Before doing so I had to destroy a secret device we had at that time called IFF (Identification, Friend or Foe). This consisted of a small box in the cockpit with, among other things, a red button on its surface covered by a flap, which we were supposed to press should the aeroplane be in danger of falling into enemy hands. We were told that an explosive device would destroy the contents beyond recognition. We were not told how big the explosion would be and whether there was any delay to allow the button pusher to escape. I didn't want to be crippled, or lose my fingers, or even perhaps my hand, so I felt just a little bit cautious.

Nobody to my knowledge had ever had to press the button. It seemed obvious, though, that the enemy weren't far away because of the disturbing bangs and phuts which were going on, so I had to do the deed. In the event, all that happened was a fizzing sound and some smoke but it sounded very destructive. I did consider destroying the aircraft as well but had no means by which to do it, so decided to leave that job to the army with their easy-to-hand demolitions. An inspection to see just what damage the enemy had done to my machine did cross my mind but in the circumstances this thought was discarded in the interests of my further good health.

My next problem was to find a way out. I found a C47 pilot who was returning to Sicily, and persuaded him to take a passenger. He was another New Zealander as it turned out, and he kindly dropped me off at my home strip. His take-off was right over the German lines where I could just about see the whites of their eyes. At any moment I expected to see holes sprouting in the bottom of the aircraft as their gunners homed in on us. Perhaps they were otherwise engaged for no holes appeared. Nevertheless one tends to feel a little exposed in a box made of thin tin. I was the first to get back and I made my report, claiming a bomber destroyed, to be shared between the three of us.

Darkness came and there was no word from the others, and we began to have grave doubts as to their safety. Because of the appalling operational conditions at the Salerno landing strip, what with its lack of any flying control, the dust, low visibility, and the signs when I left of the enemy possibly over-running the strip, I really did wonder. The next day I was amazed to find that only one of our people had returned, that three aeroplanes had collided on take-off at Salerno, and one pilot had been killed.

Out of the six aeroplanes which were involved in

that particular patrol, one had been shot down, one had been destroyed (mine), and three had been destroyed in collisions, leaving only one survivor. Quite a costly mission. Salerno was saved from being overrun by the Germans through a dash up the coast by the 8th Army.

Flight Lieutenant Bryan Young, after the war, describes in considerable detail what happened to the others in his memoirs *Beckoning Skies*, published in New Zealand. I am able only to outline the details from what he has personally told me, and from what is available in his book. It appears that except for Bill Fell and myself, the other four had all landed safely, albeit with one causing the problem described earlier. The pilots had spent the night uncomfortably on the Salerno strip. Early the next morning after being refuelled they were preparing to take off on their return journey when a dreadful accident occurred. Flight Lieutenant Goby, Bryan Young and another sergeant pilot were in a group of three waiting for the dust cloud created by other aircraft to settle sufficiently for a safe take-off when out of the dust cloud another Spitfire, the fourth one of the surviving flight, appeared at full take-off speed and crashed into them. Bill Goby was killed outright, and another Spitfire destroyed with the pilot escaping death by some miracle. Bryan Young was the only one not touched and flew the only Spitfire to return safely to Milazzo.

Bryan in his book provides considerable detail concerning the incident. As I was hospitalised shortly after, with malaria and hepatitis, I do not know what happened to the pilot who caused the mayhem, except that he did survive the war. The score for that particular action was two German bombers (Dornier 217s) downed for the loss of five Spitfires and two RAF pilots (one of whom returned after capture). The final tally must be considered in favour of the Luftwaffe!

2
Learning to Fly

From my early boyhood I had dreamed about flying and frequently spent my idle hours watching birds, especially seagulls, planing overhead in the gentle sea breezes. Books such as *Chums* and *Boy's Own Annual*, standard reading in those days, fascinated me with their stories of air battles and fighter pilots, and I determined that I should become an RAF pilot one day. Later when I saw a picture of a Spitfire on a card from my father's cigarette packet, I thought that I had never seen anything quite so beautiful, and flying one of those fighters was to be my future goal.

Unfortunately, when the Second World War started I was too young to enlist but filled in the time with the territorial Hauraki battalion as a private soldier. We spent much of 1940 in camps and on manoeuvres in the south Auckland area. The problem was that before I could enlist in the RNZAF I had to wait until I reached eighteen years of age and obtain my parents' written permission to volunteer. This last was a real problem because I had a twin brother who also wanted badly to join the air force and my mother, particularly, was not prepared to let us go.

After sustained pressure, my mother agreed to letting one of us go, and that was to be myself as I was the senior by a slight margin. In the face of an earlier flat refusal to allow my adoption of an air force career, I had chosen civil engineering as an alternative and had joined the public works department as a cadet in pursuit of that objective. After a short spell in Wellington, I was transferred to Tauranga as a draughting cadet and there I joined the territorials. Thus, my wartime career had started.

While in Tauranga in 1940 after volunteering for the RNZAF, I received a communication advising that I had to complete a course of assignments over a period of twenty-one weeks (one assignment per week) and then sit an examination. The first assignment arrived by post and to my surprise it proved to be at about sixth standard level. I completed it in about an hour and posted it off. In due course the second assignment arrived and proved just as simple. I completed that and when returning it requested all the assignments in one lot rather than waste time waiting for one a week through the post. The RNZAF proved amenable and a big packet arrived with all the remaining nineteen assignments. I managed to complete them in a week and returned them all. Silence for a while and then I was told that I would not be asked to sit the examination but to await my call-up papers. Instructions duly arrived to report to the ground training wing at Levin in February, 1941. My course was number sixteen.

Course sixteen turned out to be about thirty in number from all over New Zealand, and I was the only one to catch the Limited Express, from Frankton, for the trip to Levin. I arrived at Levin in the dark at about 4.30 am where a truck was awaiting us at the station. Others turned up at the same time from where I knew not. We were driven to the RNZAF training wing to be called henceforth ITW (initial training wing) where we ended up in the cookhouse for warmth and something to eat and drink.

When the time for work arrived (0800 hours), we were duly paraded and after an introductory talk, taken to stores to be kitted out. What a nice uniform; blue tunic and trousers, blue shirts which incidentally we had to buy ourselves and bring with us to the ITW, black tie, black socks and shoes, and blue glengarry hat. We also received a blue greatcoat which was very necessary to keep warm and a white flash to wear in front of our caps to signify aircrew. Then to work.

The daily grind started with lectures all the morning, parade ground drill all afternoon, followed by an hour's physical training, and then a three mile run. The latter was carried out with a minimum of supervision and no-one dodged so far as I knew, because no-one was prepared to give the authorities reason to dismiss one from the course for which we all had worked so hard. Everyone was fearful lest he be washed out for some reason, and all strove mightily to meet all requirements. So we studied hard, learnt our drill, and became physically fit.

On top of the academic requirements we also had to undergo a demanding medical examination before being accepted by the RNZAF. This was carried out in Hamilton by a team of specialists who tested our hearts, lungs, eyes, ears and bodies, plus medical histories which were supplied earlier. For this purpose we had to strip completely naked and move from one specialist to another to emerge at the exit somewhat demoralised. One of the general medicos had a student with him and the doctor, while carrying out his medical examination made deprecatory remarks about the physique and appearance of the patient to the student, who to give him credit, looked highly embarrassed. Some of us felt inclined to demonstrate to this arrogant fellow what it would be like to receive a punch on the nose. This was only prevented, I am sure, by the accompanying certainty of failing the medical exam.

The new recruits at Levin were separated into three groups for training; trainee pilots, trainee observers, and trainee air-gunners. The former two had a minimum qualification prerequisite of university entrance, while the latter needed no particular educational qualification. I was in the pilot's group. We studied and drilled for three weeks as juniors and then did the same again as seniors for another three weeks. Then we were put through a series of written, oral, and drill examinations to see that we had achieved the appropriate standards.

Posting to a flying station followed. I was posted with about ten others to Bell Block at New Plymouth, and duly reported there as instructed. Incidentally most of us were very proud of the LAC rank granted to us as pilot trainees. This amounted to a rank of lance-corporal in the army, and after my exalted rank of private in the army, I felt unnecessarily important.

The station at New Plymouth was called an elementary flying training school (EFTS) and was situated a small distance outside the city of New Plymouth. Again we were put through a medical board and having got so far I was fearful that they would find something wrong with me. Consequently my heart rate was at about 120 when I faced the doctor. He asked me if I had been running, and I quite untruthfully agreed that I had. He told me to sit down for a while and then come back. Sitting down worrying about my imminent dismissal didn't help, and if anything my heart rate increased. The doctor said that everything else was all right but I must return for a further check and I was to duly make an appointment. Of course I never did, and kept a mile away from any doctor. Strangely enough I heard no more about it, and suspect that the doctor wasn't a bad psychologist. At the EFTS, again, half a day was taken up with lectures and half with flying and PT (physical training).

My first ever flight occurred on 16th June 1941, in a De Havilland Tiger Moth, with Pilot Officer Clark as instructor. It was called air experience and he did all the flying while I enjoyed the view. It was great and all I thought it might be. We were not allowed to wallow in our enjoyment for long however, and the next flight followed quickly. This was called cockpit drill and effect of controls. Up we went and Pilot Officer Clark explained and demonstrated what happened when the stick (or control column) was moved, and how the rudder worked. He also demonstrated what was called a stall and I thought my flying days were numbered as my stomach flew through the top of my head and I felt that the rest of my body was to follow. My reaction was to think that my physical and nervous system were unsuitable for this sort of thing. However, we didn't do another stall, and I kept my opinions to myself. At the end of the day when we compared notes I discovered that nobody liked the stalls except for a few who had had previous experience. One of these told me to relax completely and I wouldn't have any problem. More easily said than done I thought. However, it worked and I had no further trouble during any of the heart stopping manoeuvres we had to practice later.

For seven days a week we attended lectures, undertook flying training, and did PT. I couldn't have proved a very quick learner because it took me nine and a half hours to go solo. I think that this could have been because I was trying too hard and couldn't relax. Anyway, having gone solo, I started to enjoy flying. On Saturdays and Sundays many people used to drive out to the airfield and park along the adjacent roads to watch our efforts. Of course, when crossing the fence for landings, we could see all the upturned faces, and thought that they were admiring us. On the contrary, they were getting much entertainment from the absolutely terrible touchdowns and the high bounces which followed. The sight of a Tiger Moth sailing over one's head and virtually flying into the ground and then rising in a tremendous bounce, usually followed by a series of gradually diminishing hops down the airfield until it stopped, caused much amusement I am sure. This was great fun for the watchers, and I wonder what they must have thought about the quality of New Zealand's aspiring aviators.

After three weeks of this at a junior level we were elevated to doing the same thing at a more advanced level for a further three weeks. I much later discovered that these three-week intervals were standard for air force training, not only in New Zealand, but also elsewhere in the British world. Life was still quite regimented, and in particular, we did not relate well to the pinpricking corporals who were in charge of our barracks. They were older gentlemen who saw to it that our beds were made army style, the barracks swept out and scrubbed daily, and the lights out sharp at 2200 hours. On the other hand we had a wet canteen and I had my bagpipes which were in great demand for our protest marches criticising the corporals.

We were given one weekend leave, and four of us hired a car for a two-day visit to Tauranga. The car broke down in the middle of the night at Hamilton on the return journey and we rang the RNZAF station at Bell Block to advise that we would be late returning. We were told to return as soon as possible. We thought that we had been responsible and that would be the end of the matter. However, we hadn't allowed for an adjutant who must have been an obnoxious schoolmaster in his time. We were interrogated at length, accused of deliberately stealing a few extra hours of leave, and then confined to camp until further notice. This meant reporting to the guardhouse hourly after working hours, and confinement within the station boundaries during leave periods. It remained in force until we finished our course at Bell Block.

Towards the end of our elementary flying training, we were assessed as pilots for further training on either single-engine (fighter) or multi-engine (bomber) aircraft. I received an average grade as a pilot, and an above average grade for blind flying on instruments in the Link Trainer. To my horror I saw that I was categorised as suitable for flying bombers. We were posted to the Ohakea station for service flying training there, and we duly reported for duty.

3
Service Flying Training

Ohakea was a permanent RNZAF station with substantial concrete hangars and a large grass airfield. The training aircraft were Airspeed Oxfords (a twin-engined aircraft) for bomber pilots, and Hawker Hinds (a single-engined aircraft) for fighter pilots. My first self-imposed assignment was to persuade the powers-that-be that I was most suitable for training as a fighter pilot. Accordingly, I requested a hearing, and in due course appeared before three officers to present my case. I must have been convincing because I was reassigned to Hawker Hinds, much to my relief.

The same two sets of three weekly periods of training applied at Ohakea, as it did for the rest of the country. I again went through the inevitable medical board and this time my heart behaved itself. The big difference was that this time we had to sit our wings examination after the first three weeks of lectures, PT, and flying training. Also the training was much more war orientated, such as firing machine guns and dropping bombs.

I was assigned to an instructor by the name of Flying Officer Sandy Eaton who turned out to be a very quiet chap. We got on very well, but he gave me a strong impression that he didn't trust a pupil not to kill him during flying instruction. Consequently I could feel his guiding hand on the control column at all times, and was never sure whether or not I was flying the machine. The Hawker Hind was a large aeroplane for a single seater (although there was a gunner's cockpit behind the pilot), and was very difficult to land nicely. It tended to bounce very easily. After about two hours instruction Sandy handed me over to a new instructor of a completely contrasting personality called 'Do Block' Morrison. He was a flight lieutenant, ex-RAF, and was given to ramming his tuition down the poor pupil's throat accompanied by appropriate expletives, which of course were not very complimentary to the pupil.

Anyway, we sort of got on, but I was not very happy with his battering ram approach. I was therefore very surprised one day, when after a short flight, he got out of the aircraft in the middle of the field and told me that I was on my own, and to make several circuits and landings. "And" said he, "If you break that kite, I'll break your bloody neck." I took off and thoroughly enjoyed my solo flying and landings, all of which I thought were very good.

Having successfully completed his job of pushing recalcitrants through, Do Block disappeared and I was given a Flying Officer Don Winstone as my new instructor. He had a most pleasant personality, and we got along famously. I didn't look back and I stayed with him right through the remainder of my training on Hawker Hinds. I passed out of the course marked above average as a pilot, but strangely, only average on the Link Trainer. I wonder if that might have been arranged to keep me on fighters which were perceived as not requiring the same instrument flying ability as bombers. I discovered later that I was in the top five percent for night vision.

The Hawker Hind is now a dinosaur of an aircraft, and I doubt if any are left in the world. It was manufactured by the Hawker Aircraft Company in Britain, and its type was the forerunner of the famous Hurricane fighter. Indeed the Hurricane had a very similar shape except that it was a monoplane. The Hind was a large biplane which had been in operational use on the North-West Frontier in the late 1930s. It was powered by a Rolls-Royce Kestrel engine, and had a large fixed pitch propeller. The fuselage was fabric, and the pointed nose and engine nacelle were of metal construction. It was a two seater with the pilot in the forward cockpit and a gunner in the rear cockpit with a swivel mounted Lewis machine gun.

Provision for two fixed forward firing Vickers machine guns existed alongside the pilot, although in our case, we had only one machine gun while the hole for the other remained open to the slipstream. The pilot had to climb up steps in the fuselage to reach the cockpit. The fuel system was gravity fed and required the turning of a special cock to read the quantity of fuel available. This cock always seemed to leak petrol onto the pilot's left leg which was nearly always wet with fuel as a result. We didn't worry much about that however, but did so later when we flew at night and exhaust sparks entered the cockpit through the open gun port and drifted around the cockpit. I was most alarmed at this, but no one seemed to care, and so far as I know, there were no fires from this cause, so I accepted it.

The aeroplane was quite fast (205 mph at top speed) and highly aerobatic. Two bombs could be slung under the wings so that dive-bombing could be practised. In flight, the engine was cooled by a radiator which had to be wound up and down in the slipstream by means of a wheel located at the bottom of the cockpit. This required constant attention from the pilot. The Vickers gun fired through the propeller arc, and interrupter gear prevented the gun from firing when the propeller was in the way. This gear was only effective within a certain range of engine revolutions, so that when on attack, the pilot had to work like a demon raising and lowering the radiator, keeping his engine revolutions within limits, and keeping one eye looking through the Aldis gunsight. The propeller, having no pitch control, increased or decreased revolutions every time the aeroplane dived or climbed. A number of propellers were holed or even shot off because of a failure to observe the revolution limits. Fortunately it never happened to me.

We completed our service flying training and lectures after the first three weeks and sat our wings examination, which as I recall took several three hour written papers plus oral and practical tests. Upon completion of these, those who passed were awarded their brevets (wings). Other stations held formal ceremonies and parades, but not so Ohakea. We were handed our brevets with the admonition; "Now don't think you can fly." At this time Ohakea was out of commission through flooding and we had moved to Levin where we flew from paddocks near the initial training wing where it had all started. We dined with the new recruits and took great pride in wearing our new wings.

Our remoteness from Ohakea was the probable reason for not having a parade. Our second three week period was spent on advanced flying, practising firing at a drogue, dive-bombing, aerobatics, and night flying. Finally we were either commissioned as pilot officers or promoted to sergeant. It was noted that not one from our fighter pilots course received a commission even though we took the top three places of the wings examination. All regarded as too young and undisciplined I suppose. Anyway it was quite a bone of contention and didn't help us in our later flying careers that I could see.

Although we had the usual range of accidents during our training, there were no bad crashes. The only bad incident occurred while we were night flying. A Hind caught fire on landing, and after careering down the runway as a flaming torch, ended up on its nose still burning. The pilot by the name of Ernie Mottram escaped unhurt. It appeared that the aircraft had picked up one of the burning gooseneck flares with its wing on its landing run. One incident tested me out on Hinds early in my training. Two aircraft, one with an instructor and pupil, and the other flown by myself, were flying from Ohakea to Levin one morning in bad weather when we ran into fog near Levin. This forced us down to about fifty feet. It wasn't long before I lost sight of the other aircraft, and not wishing to lose track of my position, especially as hills were very close, I flew around the streets of Levin, dodging radio aerials and such like, until I felt that the other aircraft had had sufficient time to land. I then followed the roads out to the landing area to find that sheep had been allowed on it and had to be chased away before I could alight. I landed without trouble although from a very low altitude but could only conclude that the people at the Levin strip had assumed that I had returned to Ohakea. It was the first occasion when decision-making and airmanship while flying was forced upon me.

Upon completion of our course, we were sent on leave to await our posting overseas. I returned home to Raglan and enjoyed a period free from study and service pressures. The few weeks we had passed all too quickly, and I was instructed to report to a RNZAF centre in Auckland for embarkation purposes. I and a naval seaman, Sandy McCardle, both from Raglan were farewelled in the town hall by the RSA. I said goodbye to my family on the platform of the Hamilton railway station. My poor mother was convinced, not without good reason I assumed, that she would never see her son again, but said her goodbyes with stoicism. I have never forgotten the look of agony on her face as I parted from her. The train started and I was on my way.

4

A Rough Crossing

Upon arrival in Auckland, I found friends from the same course also waiting to go overseas, and after the usual series of everlasting medical examinations and a few more booster shots in the arm, we boarded the Matson passenger liner *Monterey*, sailing to San Francisco. The United States of America was neutral then so that the ship had a numbers of tourists, and we were in effect civilian passengers. Two of us, Harry Moore and myself, had a stateroom to ourselves with all conveniences, including beds rather than bunks. We even had two portholes to our cabin, and also a steward in attendance. We were introduced to tipping early on, and a whip around was made to ensure that we received the good service for which the Matson line had a reputation. When at sea we could see on the horizon HMNZS *Leander*, acting as an unobtrusive escort presumably, to see that we reached our destination safely. "A good start" I thought, and wondered how long it would last.

We sailed across the Pacific calling in at Fiji, Pago Pago, Fanning Island where we dropped off some New Zealand troops, Hawaii, and finally arrived at San Francisco. At each stop we had a day to sightsee, and at both Fiji and Pago Pago we hired taxis for the day. At Hawaii the women of the Red Cross each took two of us to entertain, and showed us around the island, including the famous Pearl Harbor naval base of later notoriety. Altogether a very generous display of friendship.

We duly sailed into San Francisco Bay under one of the large bridges (I can't remember which) before docking at a wharf. The whole trip across the Pacific Ocean was in calm weather and we had no notion of what our future travel had in store. We were disembarked separately from the other tourist passengers, and were taken straight to the railway station where a train was awaiting our arrival. Once aboard, we were told that we were not to leave the train under any circumstances upon pain of being arrested as aliens. Actually, during the journey, some of our chaps did leave the train and there was quite a rumpus about it, but fortunately no arrests. The clandestine nature of our passage, I believe, was because the authorities did not wish the Axis powers to know that the USA was aiding Britain.

Anyway, the train travelled right up the west coast of America, through the California and Washington States, and crossed the border into Canada to complete the trip at Vancouver. We were in Vancouver for a day or two but didn't have an opportunity to see much of the city even though we were left to our own devices. The next stage commenced with our boarding a train of the Canadian National Railways. We travelled east through Jasper National Park in the Rockies. Much snow lay round about and we had an enjoyable stop at Jasper. As far as I can remember, we were on that train for about a week of constant travel, mostly through flat prairie country, with stops at Montreal and Regina. The trip was reasonably comfortable, but rather boring, particularly the prairies covered with snow.

Our destination was Halifax, which proved to be freezing cold, damp, and threatened by a dense mass of dull grey snow cloud. My general impression was of a miserable place with a miserable and disinterested people. The streets were clothed with ice, and it was difficult to keep one's footing in the shoes which we wore. We were billeted in large barracks, which were warm and dry, but the occasional parade which we were required to attend, provided problems with keeping one's feet and were finally abandoned. We would all march out on command to join the markers but would fail to stop in the right place. We just slithered on, and when a stop was achieved, usually on one's back-side, we would attempt cautiously to slide our way back into place with considerable merriment. The street trams amazed me in view of our stability problems. They were small four wheeled affairs, which seemed to travel at blind speed downhill and around corners in conditions where we couldn't keep to our feet without great care. I didn't see one accident or failure to stop at drop off points for passengers.

As I recall it, we were in Halifax for about a week left to our own devices, before we boarded a ship called *Letitia*, an erstwhile passenger liner, for our crossing of the Atlantic Ocean. Our small group was quartered in one of the holds with hammocks for beds. The ship was not clean, having been used, so we were told, to carry prisoners of war to Canada. There were insufficient hammocks for all of us, but I was fortunate to claim one for myself. Getting into it proved a very real problem, especially in a heavy sea. Firstly, one had to push apart a mass of heavy bodies already comfortably ensconced, then slide into the hammock without turning turtle and landing on a very hard deck from a height of about four feet. The attempt usually called forth a chorus of vocal protests at the disturbance, never any sympathy. After a bit of practice, one got one's head and shoulders and upper back into one end of the hammock, and holding both sides firmly open, pulled one's bottom and legs up into position. If done correctly, the hammock enfolded one's body and one was like a cocoon.

The hammock swayed backwards and forwards with the roll of the ship and only the pitching of the bow in the direction of travel was apparent to the sleeper. An unfortunate few had no hammocks and had to make do with beds on the floor of the hold trying to make themselves as secure as possible. I doubt if they slept much at all, and one poor chap fractured his leg when he was flung about during the bad weather, which was a feature of our trip across the Atlantic. We left Halifax in louring and freezing weather, and commenced our journey.

All meals, two per day, had to be collected from a galley by one of our number assigned to the job, and dished out to individuals in our part of the hold. Dirty utensils were returned to the galley but we had to wash our personal dishes in the latrine area. The crossing seemed to take a long time, but three weeks I think was the actual period. We were part of a large convoy, and followed immediately behind another liner, the *Louis Pasteur*. Boat drills were frequent in preparation for the possibility that we would be torpedoed. Indeed on more than one occasion we were informed that an attack had been made by U-boats, but how true this was I don't know, because we were not told very much.

We suffered an unvarying and uninteresting daily diet of dried apricots for most meals, and we became heartily sick of them. Then one day we were attacked with the loss of two ships. Our convoy scattered, or at least the troopships did, and we proceeded alone over a heaving and storm tossed sea. Many of us were pressed into service as lookouts, and we scoured the waves for signs of periscopes, fortunately without seeing any. It got colder and colder, and when not on duty we tried to keep warm in our hammocks. It was too rough to take exercise. It was so cold that I think our ship sailed up into the Arctic belt, but land eventually appeared, and we entered the haven of Liverpool with a sense of relief.

Many of us were not too clean as facilities were strictly limited. It was mentioned that three thousand of us were aboard whereas the ship was fitted out for only fifteen hundred. Before we left the ship, we were inspected for lice, and some head shaving was carried out. Eventually we disembarked straight on to a train which left for an unknown destination. This turned out to be Bournemouth in the south of England. On the way we were given tea and biscuits. The latter defied all attempts at ingesting them. They resisted biting, breaking, and dunking. We jumped on them, hammered them, and scraped them with little discernable effect. Only by soaking them for a long time in one's hot tea could one get any sustenance from them. I have never seen them again since but consider that they would be ideal for hungry children. After our very restricted diet aboard the ship I wondered what our first meal in England would be like. I had never been in another country so did not know what to expect. Our first hot meal consisted of one course, which was a great shock to a well-fed New Zealander who especially enjoyed his dessert. *No sweet?!* What sort of society did they have in Britain? I later discovered that my terrible fears were unfounded, thank the Lord.

5
Action at Last

It was 1941 and winter was well advanced. Britain was in dire straits with its back still to the wall, and on its own. Christmas was coming. Life proved to be spartan. Four of us were billeted in an empty boarding house without heating, minimal lighting, and no facilities for cooking or even making a cup of tea. We each had a wire wove mattress, three padded cushions called biscuits, and three blankets. The three biscuits were pushed together to form some sort of mattress, but gaps between them could not be avoided however careful one was when turning over during the night. We spread our blankets on top and froze. Sleep was impossible with the Arctic breeze flowing up through the gaps in the biscuits. We put newspapers under the mattress which stopped the draughts and meant we had only the insufficiency of three blankets to worry about. Daylight arrived at about 0900 hours, and it was pitch-black night-time again at about 1600 hours. There was a complete blackout at night, and what few vehicles operated did so with a feeble glimmer from heavily shielded headlights.

The location of our billets was Boscombe, a suburb of Bournemouth. This place had a special significance for me as it was where my father was billeted when with the 1st NZEF while waiting to go to France. He survived wounding and gassing. I tried hard to imagine his walking the streets and attending shows. Everything looked so antique that it could easily have not altered since his time, 1916 I think. We had to parade at 0900 hours for a roll call, and after that we had the whole day to ourselves. Much of the time we spent sightseeing and attending the local cinemas. A film started at 1430 hours and finished at 1600 hours so that we entered the theatre in daylight and came out in inky darkness. One would make one's way down the street to the bus stop by feeling blindly in front so as to avoid unseen obstacles, and frequently one's fingers would encounter someone's face. There would be mutual apologies all round as one would pass on to return to the billets for another miserably cold night.

We soon became terribly bored by the lack of action, and approached New Zealand's high commissioner in London, Mr Bill Jordan, to see if he could move things along. The only result was a move up the coast to Hastings just across the English Channel from France. There we had a room on the thirteenth floor of an unfinished hotel and found the climb up the stairs to our room quite a deterrent. A complaint to the authorities only produced wry smiles and advice that it was a nuisance but it would keep us fit and healthy. We retaliated by feeding seagulls outside our window. The massed gulls spread their deposits over the parading troops below. It wasn't long before we were formally ordered to stop feeding the gulls.

Hastings is famous for its battle where the Normans conquered the Saxons and King Harold took an arrow in his eye at a spot called Battle, just outside Hastings itself. It is also near Rye, one of the ancient Cinque Ports. Of considerable interest to me were quite a number of bullet holes in the walls of some of the town buildings. I was told upon enquiry that these were the result of strafing attacks by Messerschmitt fighters. So what we had heard about firing at civilian targets was true. Hastings was very near to the French coast and we witnessed a number of naval and air actions in the Channel. This only increased our desire to do something positive.

As time went on we approached Bill Jordan again, and action occurred at last. We were posted to the RAF station Hullavington in Wiltshire, near a small town called Chippenham. Imagine our surprise to find the NZ Army there. These chaps were a forestry unit of the 2nd Echelon, and involved with local forestry activities. We passed them in the bus on our way to the airfield and they showed annoyance when we shouted friendly insults as we went by. Of course they didn't know that we were countrymen. Flying started again, and we were introduced first of all to the Miles Master Mk 1, a low winged monoplane powered by a Rolls-Royce Kestrel motor (the same as we had on Hawker Hinds), and with retractable undercarriage, variable speed propellers, and under wing flaps. They were very fast and were our first taste of a modern aeroplane.

Of great interest to us was the presence of a Hurricane fighter which would be available for us to fly later on. This I did at the end of our course, and gained an impression that I was flying a rocket, so great was the difference between a modern fighter and a training aircraft. Our training course, which was really a conversion onto modern aircraft after our experience on the earlier pre-war machines, prepared us for the next phase, which was to be at an operational training unit.

Our stay at Hullavington was most pleasant, with rugby, football and indoor basketball to keep us fit. Such things do not last of course, and upon completion of the course we were posted to 55 Operational Training Unit (OTU) at Annan in Dumfrieshire, Scotland. This OTU was equipped with Mk 1 Hurricane fighters, a disappointment for me because I was aware that there were Spitfire OTUs. Although I was unaware of it at the time, Annan was quite near an old Peart hometown called Alston, in Cumberland. As seemed to be the norm, even in the UK, our course was made up of two three-week intervals, the first of which was regarded as junior and the second senior.

In the first three weeks we learned to fly the Hurricane as an aeroplane until we were thoroughly familiar with its idiosyncrasies and flying characteristics. This included formation flying, cloud flying, aerobatics, night flying, and tail chasing. At the end of this we flew the aeroplane as an extension of ourselves. The tail chasing was quite exciting. It consisted of several aeroplanes flying in line astern following a leader. The leader who was usually an instructor, flew all around the sky, up cloud faces, through cloud holes, twisting and turning, until the following aeroplanes were thoroughly disorientated.

Then flying became truly automatic. Of course lectures were also part of the course, and these were given at night over a range of subjects. Most of the day was spent flying, every day, seven days a week, mostly irrespective of the weather. The second three weeks was spent on learning to use the Hurricane as an offensive weapon and gun platform. We had four machine guns in the wings used for practice firing at drogues and ground targets. The largest proportion of the time was spent on dogfighting and navigation. This latter was important because the British Isles were not noted for their good flying conditions. The weather was frequently bad with a low ceiling and low visibility. When fine weather did prevail, there was usually a heavy haze which severely restricted visibility except at altitude.

It was during this period that I had my first accident, which could have been fatal. I was dogfighting with an opponent who was on my tail. To get rid of him I dived vertically into cloud, flew in the cloud for a short distance, and then climbed vertically up to my former altitude expecting to find my opponent lower down, looking for me. I was rolling out on the top of my climb still looking for my enemy, when to my horror I saw him flying right into me, not having seen me. I immediately stopped my roll and hauled the nose down inverted. There was a bang and the other Hurricane roared over the top of me. We both returned to base where I expected to see a lot of damage, but I had escaped with a score right across the bottom of my radiator. The propeller of the other aeroplane was damaged. The authorities said nothing except that a better lookout had better be kept in future. The second part of our course was completed at a satellite base at Longtown near Carlisle, in Cumberland.

We did have some leisure time and at Annan we indulged in trout fishing, rabbit shooting, and rambling per the courtesy and generosity of the local squire. Longtown is situated close to the Lake District and I was struck by the beauty of this particular part of Britain. More can be seen from the air than from the ground, and I used to marvel at the large and beautiful mansions set amid magnificent forests and lakes. I imagined the garden parties which must have been held there by the landed gentry. I was impressed and surprised when someone told me that much of the land was owned and administered by the Church of England. Bishops apparently had residences there. I must study up the history of England a bit more, I thought to myself, but the opportunity to do so did not come my way.

6
Spitfires

Our course at 55 OTU was completed at the end of June 1942, and I was posted to 610 Spitfire Squadron stationed at Ludham near Norwich. Coltishall was our main RAF base, and Ludham was one of two satellites. The other, the name of which I forget, was used by Westland Whirlwinds, twin-engine single-seat fighters. This was 610's partner in protecting our sector from enemy attack. The Whirlwinds did not prove very satisfactory in their role and were eventually phased out of use, but this left 610 with a lone task which kept it quite busy. I travelled alone to Ludham by train with all my gear, wondering what it would be like on an operational squadron. The awful truth gradually dawned on me that from now on things were for real, and I pondered on what the future might hold for me. Would I be an early casualty; an easy target for some German ace, before I could get enough experience to look after myself? All my past reading on the matter confirmed the likelihood of that scenario. It was a traumatic and sobering thought.

A vehicle met me and one other sergeant pilot at the railway station, and we were delivered to the headquarters of the squadron where we duly reported for duty. The other sergeant pilot had the rare surname of Brown, and we became good friends. I do not know if he survived the war, but this is unlikely as 610 Squadron received a severe mauling later. Everything seemed to be housed in Nissen huts, semi-circular corrugated metal structures. Our billets were in one such, and we each had a room to ourselves. The sergeants' mess was a comfortable establishment in another Nissen hut.

The meals were adequate and generally excellent. The aerodrome was quite some distance away and had to be reached by vehicle, usually driven by an attractive WAAF. It had two sealed runways which ran through a farmed area, presumably to make it hard to define for enemy bombers and fighters. Two dispersal buildings were situated close to the runways, one for A Flight and the other for B Flight. The aircraft, beautiful looking Spitfires, were spaced around the dispersal huts.

It was now summer and the weather was fine and warm, and the pilots sat outside the dispersal in armchairs, reading, listening to records, or dozing, while awaiting a sudden call for action, called a 'scramble'. I well remember a later occasion when we were lounging in chairs or lying on the grass awaiting a scramble, the gramophone was scratching out some sort of rubbishy music. The only decent record in my exalted opinion was a thing titled *Begin the Beguin* (forgive the spelling). This I played at every opportunity until one day my esteemed colleagues broke it over my head. Then ensued a very smashing session, and we had to acquire a new set of records. I forget whether or not the musical standards of my fellow pilots improved as a consequence.

I was surprised to find during my introduction to the squadron members that we had no commanding officer. No explanation was offered, and I had to assume that he had been killed in action (a rather alarming thought as things must be really dicey when a CO gets killed), or perhaps he had been promoted to higher office, ethereal or physical. Anyway, I was given to understand that I would get no flying until a new CO was appointed. My duties until that event would be those of the duty pilot, which entailed spending my time in the control tower processing all incoming and outgoing aircraft traffic. I did get a great view of Spitfires taking off and landing, and had as a diversion the presence of three WAAFs who dealt with the telephone exchange. As the sole male I was well looked after. I was, however, beginning to become quite frustrated with my lot when the new CO arrived.

He turned out to be Squadron Leader 'Johnnie' Johnson, later to become the top scoring British ace. This was his first squadron command. He presented a most likeable personality, and one automatically felt at ease in his presence. He had with him a beautiful golden retriever dog, and true to type drove a sports car. The dog accompanied him everywhere except in his aeroplane. When the squadron was away on a sortie the dog would await his return at the dispersal. Most unfortunately, the dog was run over by the dispersal truck and killed. The WAAF driver was most upset, but the CO couldn't have been nicer about it. He did not replace his dog though, at least while I was on the squadron.

Immediately after his arrival I was called to flying again, and I became aware that more training was in store. This consisted predictably of learning to fly and fight with the Spitfire to a level acceptable to my flight commander. I was attached to A Flight where I had to familiarize myself with our sector of Britain down to the finest detail so that I remembered every landmark, including churches, prominent buildings, and other features. This required flying over the territory again and again until the memory was adequately imprinted and the necessity and wisdom of this was brought home later.

Then came twilight flying until one was considered proficient at landing in semi-dark conditions when it is hard to judge heights and distances. This was followed by night flying when I was required to become proficient at taking off and landing, and finding my way about with the minimum of lighting. The flare path lights for instance would be switched on for just sufficient time to take off, and upon return, to approach and touch the ground, and then they would be switched off in case an enemy intruder was around. Having reached the required standard of proficiency in all these things, I was declared fully operational and was given operational tasks. These were initially carried out as a number two to a more experienced pilot, as we always flew in pairs.

I well remember my first flight in a Spitfire. After having familiarized myself with all the controls and recorded handling characteristics, plus any other written material I could lay hands on, I had the cockpit layout and various flying idiosyncrasies explained after I had strapped myself into the cockpit. The Spitfire was a Mk V aircraft with two cannons and four machine guns as its armament, and a Mk 46 Rolls-Royce Merlin engine. The Spitfire, like all single seat fighters at that time, had no dual version, so the new pilot had to rely on advice for his first flight. This wasn't as bad as it might seem provided that care was exercised to adhere strictly to the standard rules for take-off and landing. While most first take-offs and landings were safely executed, by no means could they be called good, for the Spitfire had a reputation for being difficult to land.

When ready, I started the engine, taxied to the take-off position on the runway and received permission to take off. I opened the throttle and the aeroplane went right round in a circle in spite of my best endeavours to keep it straight. This was my first lesson on the power of the engine which needed a carefully controlled throttle opening for take-off. The propeller transmits its power to the aeroplane which cannot roll around in the opposite direction, so it swings badly as a result. I throttled back and lined up again, this time opening the throttle more slowly, and having no trouble in keeping the aircraft straight. It was much more powerful and faster than anything I had flown before, and after spending some time getting used to the sensitive controls at a safe altitude, I returned to the aerodrome and made my landing without mishap. With its narrow undercarriage and long nose, it was quite a difficult aeroplane to land, and bounces, together with rocking from side to side after touchdown, were the hallmark of the inexperienced pilot.

My first operational sortie was what we called a

'Jim Crow'. This consisted of a section (pair) of Spitfires flying low across the North Sea to the Dutch coast, and then flying south down the coast to locate enemy shipping and anything else worth reporting. The coast was dotted with flak ships and small craft, and having checked the length of coast for anything new, the section would fly back and when close to the English coast would gain altitude and report what had been observed. If a ship was seen an attack was in order, but flak ships were avoided. In general it wasn't a bad introduction to operations as the danger of combat was not very great, but on occasion enemy aircraft were encountered, and shipping was attacked with consequential return fire.

My first trip was with an experienced number one, and we just looked around. On later such trips we did attack boats and a flak ship. We caught both types unprepared so escaped the dense return fire that a flak ship could put up. Another type of operation, called a 'Rhubarb' was to fly low inland in bad weather looking for trains, troop concentrations, military traffic, and anything else worth shooting up with our cannons and machine guns. This type of operation was invariably carried out in bad weather with a low cloud ceiling so that interception by enemy fighters was difficult. Other operations involved patrols over convoys in the North Sea, interception of incoming enemy aircraft, and general patrolling of our territory. We also patrolled on moonlit nights when enemy bombers were carrying out raids, but it proved extraordinarily difficult to see another aircraft under these conditions.

Another fairly frequent operation was to assist our bombers down through murky weather and guide them to an aerodrome. We saved quite a number of damaged bombers this way. This type of operation required all of the knowledge we had of our sector as explained earlier, because after interception, we would have the bomber formate on us for descent through cloud to a very low level below the cloud ceiling, and we needed to know exactly where we were at all times. Not infrequently, the countryside would be shrouded in fog, and we would still be required to assist the bombers down. I remember once locating my position by the arrangement of church steeples and other landmarks sticking up through the murk. One could actually land through it with the use of a flare path. By this time I was feeling a lot more confident flying a Spitfire.

The occasion arrived when we moved down to West Malling near London to carry out what were called 'Balbos', which were in effect fighter sweeps over France with the aim of drawing up enemy fighters. My first sweep was as part of the Dieppe raid and its aftermath. I was at the tail of my squadron, the place allotted to the most inexperienced pilots, and of course the most vulnerable. We were part of a wing made up of three squadrons of Spitfires, led by a wing commander.

All of the pilots participating were briefed on the purpose of the operation, which was to draw into combat as many enemy fighters as possible. I couldn't help noticing that many of the senior pilots were quite well decorated, so presumably had been in combat on many occasions. The briefing went on to predict how many German fighters might be expected to react to our presence. I was not a little alarmed to hear that some forty-plus were expected from Abbeville (a German fighter base), another twenty-plus from somewhere else, and other contributions from all over the place. And the total number of Spitfires attracting all this attention would be thirty-six. Even more alarming to a sprog like myself was a prediction that up to twenty-five percent casualties were likely.

I looked along the line of chaps next to me and wondered who was due for the chop. The station CO, a group captain, then said that we could smoke. I didn't smoke then, but couldn't help noticing that many of the decorated officers did, and that when they lit up, their hands were shaking so much that some appeared to have difficulty getting the match to their cigarette. After a big drag on the cigarette, they appeared to relax and the shakes disappeared. I thought to myself, "there must be something in cigarette smoking after all", and so I started. I needed it after that demonstration.

We took off in formations of twelve aeroplanes at a time, which was a new experience for me. However, wc were well versed in formation flying and the take-off was no different really. The whole wing assembled on its way over the Channel and there were constant exhortations to the 'tail-end Charlies' like me to keep up and not lag behind where enemy fighters could pick us off singly. This keeping up was far from easy and the poor tail end Charlie had to use much more throttle than the others, and therefore more fuel, so was worried all the time whether he would have enough fuel to get home. Anyway, we new-chums were told that if somehow we became separated from the rest of the squadron, we were to high tail it for home.

At that time the Germans had Messerschmitt 109s and Focke-Wulf 190s, both of which were more than a match for our Spitfire Mk Vs. I recall having great trouble keeping up with the rest, and seeing the vapour trails of enemy fighters weaving patterns well above us. The VHF radio was alive with instructions about manoeuvres to counter enemy attack and we were weaving about madly. We were ordered to break port or break starboard as the enemy fighters made their attacks on us, and while all of this went on, I didn't see a thing except the aforementioned vapour trails.

Finally we made our collective way home where pilots made their reports upon arrival back at base. I was most surprised to hear some claiming victories, especially as I had not even seen an enemy fighter. I was even more amazed when my section leader said that a FW 190 had fired at me. This was my first experience of combat, and I then realized how vulnerable a new pilot could be until he learned how to vary his eye focus while in the air to pick up objects at widely varying distances. It was extremely difficult to see the specks which could be other aeroplanes at a distance in a blue sky with no background. It was a skill only obtained with much practice, and when I finally mastered it it was like opening up a new world. I started to see at a far-off distance objects such as other aeroplanes, and could follow what was going on when we did get into action. I am sure that many of our losses were due to a pilot's failure to master this skill.

Certainly one of the most dangerous periods was when one was a 'green' pilot, another being a failure to remain fully alert at all times. I also encountered another most alarming phenomenon while participating in fighter sweeps over France in the winter. The atmosphere has layers of relatively warm and cold air even at great altitude, and with one's fighter cooling to a temperature somewhere around minus twenty or thirty degrees centigrade and passing through a suddenly warm and humid layer, frost forms over the windscreen and the whole perspex canopy in a small fraction of a second. So from being able to see what was going on one second, one was completely blind the next. With enemy fighters waiting to attack this was an appalling situation to be in, and when I encountered it, I was frightened out of my wits.

Upon thinking about it, I concluded that the opposition would hopefully experience exactly the same thing. One could only imagine an enemy fighter attacking only to find himself suddenly blind as well as his target. I suppose a collision could have been on the cards. All the above learning experiences started my career as a RAF fighter pilot. There was quite a large element of luck in the early stages.

Besides the duties I have already described, we participated in the activities of convoy patrols and bomber cooperation. The convoy patrol, of which we did many, consisted of flying around designated convoys in the North Sea to prevent attacks by low flying ME 109s or JU 88s. It was tiring work circling a convoy, usually in bad weather, and being shot at by the very vessels we were trying to protect if we came too close. They seemed to have plenty of ammunition to expend, and didn't hesitate to let loose with 20 mm Oerlikons and heavier anti-aircraft guns. It was amazing how much firepower those ships had. I have personally seen them shoot down one of our own aircraft within sight of the home port, and our opinion of the aircraft recognition capabilities of the navy and the merchant navy didn't bear repeating. While others encountered enemy aircraft, I didn't, and I regarded convoy patrols as a bore, although risky because of AA fire from our friendly ships.

Bomber cooperation took two forms. One consisted of acting the part of the attacking fighter to give the bomber pilot practice in evasion techniques, and the air gunners target practice under active service conditions. Quite a number of bomber stations were nearby, and we gave a service to Wellington bombers, Halifaxes, and later to Lancasters. I was most surprised at the manoeuvrability of the latter. The Lancaster pilots could throw those big four-engined machines around like fighters. I wondered how the crew felt. The second form which I have mentioned already, consisted of helping lost bombers down through cloud and bad weather conditions and leading them to a suitable airfield.

Our detailed local knowledge and ability to fly in all weather conditions was often put to use. We would climb up through the muck under the directions of the controller, and would intercept the lost or damaged bomber. It was then our duty to allow the bomber to formate on us while we descended through the cloud and found the nearest bomber aerodrome for it. Then it was over to the bomber pilot to make his landing. It was not easy by any means as the bomber always flew at a much lower speed than the Spitfire and we would have to throttle back so that the bomber could formate.

Coming back from one such trip, I encountered dense fog right down to ground level, and had to dodge church steeples and other obstacles sticking up through the mist to make my home landing. We seemed to do this without mishap, such was our knowledge of the local area. By and large life wasn't bad, and we always had a comfortable bed to sleep in, good meals, and a social life available in the nearest town. We did have the odd loss but not too often.

7

From Scotland to Spain

Life as a member of 610 Squadron was varied and as fighter pilots we encountered many risks. Probably as a test of my night flying training on Spitfires while I was with the squadron, I was pulled out of bed at approximately 0400 hours on a cold and wet morning and told to carry out a search of the North Sea for a dinghy carrying downed airmen. The weather was terrible with a gale force wind and storm clouds. It was very dark. I took off in my Spitfire and headed out to sea trying to keep a lookout while the controller vectored me in various directions. It was really impossible to see anything as small as an inflatable dinghy in the pitch-blackness and driving rain. Suddenly it became even blacker, so dark that I could hardly see my gloves on the control column, and it became even more imperative to fly by my instruments which had a phosphorescent glow under the beams of ultra violet lamps located at each side of the cockpit. These lamps, rather than the usual lighting, were essential to allow the pilot to retain his night vision for combat.

Almost immediately violent turbulence commenced with lightning discharges and St Elmo's fire linking extremities of the aircraft. I had flown right into a cumulonimbus cloud. "To hell with trying to find a dinghy in this" I thought, and I completed a slow and careful 180 degree turn while being violently thrown around. When I finally got clear of the turbulence, I called the controller on my VHF and reported the impossible weather conditions as so bad that the task could not be accomplished. I advised him that if I proceeded he was likely to have a further search for another dinghy on his hands. I was recalled and thankfully arrived back at base without further incident. I still wonder why I was sent out on such a night, except to further my night flying experience. It was quite a traumatic episode, and very lonely.

Unfortunately such experiences were not uncommon. Another occurred when I was sent to Drem airport near Edinburgh to pick up an item for our CO. The famed Dieppe raid was due to start, and I didn't want to miss it. Therefore, having flown to Drem in bad weather (which appeared to be the norm in the wintertime), I was concerned the next morning to find that the cloud had really lowered to ground level, and I couldn't see the end of the aerodrome. The weather report for the area through which I was to fly was reasonable, and I decided to proceed (they didn't close airports to us). My take-off was normal and I flew straight into cloud. As there were hills just south of Drem, I kept on climbing to clear them. Once in cloud, I had to climb out of the murk in order to descend into clear air nearer to my destination.

There were only very primitive guidance systems in those days. Icing set in while I climbed and the aircraft grew heavy and difficult to control. At 30,000 feet I emerged from the cloud heavy with ice and facing a solid mass of cumulonimbus going up to 35,000 feet at least. I was faced with flying ahead into further turbulent cloud with an ice-laden aircraft hard to control, and no way of returning to my starting point. There was also a fuel problem after the climb. After consultation with my ground control, it was decided that my only recourse was to bale out. After receiving the usual pleasantries and good luck wishes, I carried out the drill for leaving the aircraft by parachute. I had my harness undone and was taking deep breaths of pure oxygen preparative to a long free fall from 30,000 feet, when I flew over a hole through which I could see the ground.

Without waiting, in case the hole closed in, I flung the Spitfire into a vertical dive through the narrow tunnel. Ice flew off as I went down, and with the improved control I could remain within the confines of the hole by aileron turning. I pulled out at high speed at 500 feet in pouring rain and low cloud. I could see the ground and didn't intend losing it again, particularly as there was no further high ground to the south. Suddenly something flicked past my port wing, and then something again. I had flown right into the Newcastle balloon barrage set up to protect the city from attack by low flying enemy aircraft. A quick look at my map showed me its shape and I turned north to fly out of it, keeping a wary eye open for further cables. I was flying at my lowest safe speed of about 180 mph. When I judged that I was clear I turned inland and south again. After a while a cable flicked past and upon consultation of my map I decided that I must have hit the Middlesborough barrage a little further to the south.

While flying between the two I had passed over an aerodrome, so having had enough of flying through bad weather and encountering balloon barrages, I decided to find the aerodrome again and land there. This I managed in pouring rain without further incident and placed myself at the mercy of the people there for the night. I telephoned Drem to let them know that I had landed safely and settled down to await the next day.

I took off in the morning and returned to Ludham only to find myself in dire trouble. I had failed to advise the London radio centre of my safe landing, and Drem certainly had not, something I had expected them to do. Before deciding to parachute, both London and Drem had been talking to me, and London had dispatched both the army on land, and the RAF Air Sea Rescue at sea who had been looking for me in the most shocking weather. I felt dreadful about it and received a reprimand, which in the circumstances I accepted as justified.

On 17th August I flew to West Malling with the squadron to participate in the Dieppe Raid. There, we lost some pilots, one of whom was Sergeant South Creagh, an Australian, and I had my first involvement in a dog fight with the enemy. After Dieppe, we spent quite some time at West Malling and Biggin Hill fighter stations carrying out sweeps and other offensive sorties over France. These involved much more in the way of attack by enemy fighters than our previous visits to the Dutch coast and inland from our base at Ludham.

By October 1942 I had just become reasonably confident that I could become a useful fighter pilot when the squadron received instructions to move to the top of Scotland to a place called Castletown for a rest. Castletown is situated between Thurso and Wick, not far south from the Orkney Islands, and we were flown up there in an antiquated Handley Page Harrow, which looked like a First World War bomber. However, we arrived there safely. Shortly after our arrival, I was called by the CO, Johnnie Johnson, who advised me that I was being recommended for a commission. The initiating moves were made, and I was expected to receive an interview with the air officer commanding in due course. At the same time a call was made for volunteers to serve in Malta and I, feeling that I hadn't earned a rest, applied. As seems to be usual, those that volunteered were not selected, but others, including some married men, were. I suggested that I could take the place of one of these, and this time I was successful. Two of us were chosen. To my surprise we were given our postings immediately, and my potential commission went out the window. This did not trouble me at the time, but I later found that this was a mistake.

I had to abandon my gear and personal belongings, which had not yet arrived from Ludham, and with the other chap whose name I forget, we departed with only what we stood up in plus our flying gear. We had blue uniforms with white roll-necked sweaters and nothing else. We changed trains at Inverness at the dead of night and in pitch-blackness, and in the transfer my flying gear was stolen. This included helmet, radio gear, goggles, parachute and dinghy plus mae west, all in a parachute bag. It was never recovered but my helmet turned up in India years later. Perhaps the thief had some shred of conscience after all. After a number of confrontations with officious military police who objected to our informal attire, we finally arrived at Lyneham, which was a special departure point for parts unknown. The same evening we boarded a Liberator bomber bound for Gibraltar. So started my career in the Middle East.

To return to Castletown for a moment, we flew patrols over the naval base of Scapa Flow, and scouted areas around the Scottish coast. It was autumn and the weather was abysmal. The country and the coast were rugged in the extreme, and the cloud ceiling generally lay below the nearby mountains and hills. Long tendrils of mist descended right down to the sea, so that flying in these conditions gave the impression that one was wending a way through a forest of misty trunks over a dull grey carpet of sea. It was calm at the time. The sun did not shine for the whole six-week period that I was there, and I developed a hearty admiration for what can only be the hardiness of the Scottish race. Unfortunately my flying logbook was with my gear which was so late in arriving, so I have no record of my flying in the north of Scotland. I was issued with a new logbook when I reached Gibraltar and there is a hiatus in my flying record.

The flight to Gibraltar over the Bay of Biscay and down the coast of Portugal was at night, and fortunately uneventful. The Liberator was stripped bare; we had no seats, and just lay on the cold metal floor, making ourselves as comfortable as we could. There were no windows so that if there was anything to see, we couldn't satisfy our curiosity. Perhaps that was just as well, as enemy night fighters did patrol over the Bay of Biscay trying to catch transport aircraft such as ours, and they were sometimes successful. Gibraltar turned out to be a large rock attached by a narrow isthmus to Spain.

We disembarked from our aircraft in bright sunlight and a warm temperature, quite a contrast to what we had left in Britain. We were shown our billets in a shed on the side of the aerodrome runway which was a sealed strip running roughly north and south closely against the towering walls of the Rock. Our first reaction was to note the adverse change in the quality of our new accommodation. Nothing like the comfortable barracks we had enjoyed in Britain. For a while we had time to spare, and this we spent exploring the main township of Gibraltar. The business district consisted mainly of cafes, drinking dens, and small shops. This was densely populated, predominately by Spanish citizens who daily entered Gibraltar in the early morning, and returned across the border to their homes in Spain in the evening. Right on the border was a settlement called La Linea which I should like to have visited but couldn't.

Further across was the Spanish town of Algeciras, which was in its turn close to suburban hills that overlooked Gibraltar and its airfield. The famous apes of Gibraltar put in an appearance for our benefit, and to me they looked just like ordinary quite tame monkeys. Sharing our spacious accommodation in the empty shed were a number of sergeant pilots and we all kept together on our nightly visits to the fleshpots of Gibraltar. I teamed up with two in particular, Larry Cronin, an Australian, and Bill Caldecott, an Englishman. We had been told that we were to join an aircraft carrier from which we would eventually take off with our Spitfires to fly on to Malta. This sounded exceedingly dicey, but also exciting. However, upon my arrival at Gibraltar, we had been asked what aeroplanes we had flown. I, rather foolishly, admitted that I had flown Hurricane fighters. This was greeted with an enthusiasm which, at the time, I could not explain.

Apparently Hurricane pilots were exceedingly scarce in Gibraltar, and I found myself detained for the purpose of flying a Hurricane Mk 2 (twin cannons in each wing) as a night fighter defence of the Rock. The others (except Cronin and Caldecott) went their way, presumably to Malta, and were never seen or heard of by us again. They were in all probability killed in action. While we were at Gibraltar, large quantities of war materials were arriving at the airstrip and it was obvious that something was afoot. We were conscripted into helping to uncrate and assemble Spitfires, and then to test fly them.

This wasn't as complex as it might seem, as each crate contained a fully completed fuselage including the engine, two wings, and a propeller. Our team, which included engine fitters and riggers, pulled out the fuselage onto jigs, and then attached the wings which contained the undercarriage. This was lowered, and then only the propeller had to be fitted. The aeroplane was then ready for the attention of specialist fitters, riggers, electricians and other experts in the electronic fields. When all was ready we tested the aeroplane in flight. Remarkably, I cannot remember an occasion when trouble was experienced.

It wasn't long before the whole aerodrome and its surrounds became cluttered with aircraft, tanks, vehicles, and other warlike equipment. With their undoubted observers of all these goings-on from across the border, the Germans must have been aware that something was up. During this time I tested and flew my Hurricane during the day, and sat at readiness during the night. Had the Germans decided to bomb Gibraltar, I could not have provided a very effective defence on my own at night, but we did have a good defence with the Spitfires during the day. I prayed that I wouldn't have to take off at night in an aircraft I didn't have a lot of confidence in. Days passed, and no attempt was made by the Germans to attack Gibraltar, much to my relief.

One day we returned to our billets in the evening to find armed guards everywhere challenging our presence. This was quite a shock, especially when they seriously threatened us with being shot if we didn't identify ourselves satisfactorily. We were not amused. The next day, landings were made in Algeria and French Morocco. At this time I saw a demonstration of irresponsibility by the navy, which angered me. From the aerodrome we could see across the Gibraltar Straits to North Africa, and also through the Straits out into the Atlantic Ocean. A convoy only a few miles from Gibraltar was being patrolled by a Catalina flying boat, a unique type of machine which could hardly be confused with any German aircraft of the same type in the vicinity, especially so close to a major British base. Suddenly there was a burst of anti-aircraft fire from the ships, and the Catalina went down in flames.

A quite indefensible lapse in aircraft recognition by the navy which already had a very bad reputation for this type of thing. I could see no mitigating circumstances at all, and it certainly didn't do much for inter-service relations. The incident must have been hushed up because we heard nothing further about it.

8

North Africa

The 'Torch' operation consisting of landings in
Algeria and French Morocco in November 1942
went off quite well with 81 Squadron landing at
Maison Blanche airport near Algiers after a one
way flight, there being no way of returning to
Gibraltar once committed. The Maison Blanche
airport was supposed to have been captured before
the arrival of our fighters, but it was found still in
Vichy French hands. Some French Dewoitine
fighters were circling the airfield upon 81's arrival,
and one of these dived and fired at one of the
Spitfires coming in to land. Immediate refuelling of
the Spitfires commenced from drums which had
been dropped on the airfield, while the CO,
Squadron Leader 'Razz' Berry, argued with the local
French commander, each telling the other that he
was his prisoner. The argument was settled by the
appear-ance of a British tank, whereupon the
Frenchman conceded defeat.

After refuelling was completed, a section of the
squadron took off and chased the Dewoitines away.
These presumably had to crash somewhere because
there were no alternative airstrips available to them
as far as we knew. No qualms were felt about their

welfare. After a hectic few days at Maison Blanche, 81 Squadron proceeded up the coast, finally arriving at Bône, a small port near the borders of Tunisia. It was at this stage that Larry Cronin and Bill Caldecott were posted to 81 Squadron, but I was not. My consternation was great and my disappointment bitter. Why should I have been left out of things? Presumably I was to stay in Gibraltar carrying out useless night fighter patrols, but we had been told nothing. I decided that I would go with them, and together we flew replacement Spitfires on the long trip to Maison Blanche airport right next to the city of Algiers.

By this time the Germans had reacted to the invasion and an unpleasant period followed with night and daylight bombing raids. Besides high explosive bombs, the field was saturated with anti-personnel butterfly bombs, and booby traps such as fake tins of food, pens, and watches. When knocked or disturbed by picking up, these devices exploded with sufficient force to maim or severely wound. While few soldiers or airmen were deceived, except by accident, many children, chiefly of Arab extraction were. They roamed the area at night and fell victim to the devices, especially the attractive ones. The Luftwaffe also dropped specially designed spikes to puncture the tyres of aircraft taking off or landing, and a number of crashes occurred as a result of these. In addition aircraft were put out of service.

Dining and sleeping facilities were non-existent and we had to pick up what we could from boxes of invasion rations which were available, fourteen men per box. The rations consisted of tinned meat, tinned fruit, a mixture of powdered milk and tealeaves, chocolate, and cigarettes. No sleeping facilities were available, and in any case it wasn't healthy to stay anywhere near the airport at night. At dusk, before the bombing started, we would disperse to ditches as far away from the airport as we could reasonably get, and there we would settle down for the night. A ditch wasn't a bad substitute for a slit trench. Although the night hours were punctuated by exploding sticks of bombs and continuous anti-aircraft fire throughout the dark hours, I, and I am sure the others too, managed to sleep quite soundly, even though on one occasion I selected a spot right next to a Bofors gun which fired continuously throughout most of the night.

I used to select my sleeping spot with care, having noted the fall of bombs the night before, and having assessed whether an attack was likely on the anti-aircraft defences. Our only real grumble was that we had no wet weather clothing, and consequently suffered from dampness when it rained, which it did quite often. Things gradually settled down, the airfield was cleaned up, and the bombing countered by the use of night fighters. Larry, Bill, and I flew on to Bône, much further along the coast towards Tunisia to join 81 Squadron.

My arrival at Bône in a Spitfire Mk VC (tropical-ised version) was rather traumatic. Larry, Bill, and I arrived over Bône to see a battered looking airfield, seemingly a swamp, covered in bomb craters and surprisingly, there was quite a lot of rain at that time. The aerodrome had two tar-sealed runways, which looked extremely unusable. The sky was grey and overcast with a cloud ceiling of about 3,000 feet. We all landed, and taxied to the dispersal area where other Spitfires were parked in what was a field of mud. An aircraftman sat on my tail while I taxied where directed to a spot in the mud and stopped the engine. This tail sitting was essential to prevent the Spitfire upending onto its nose because of the drag through the mud. My meagre clothing and few personal possessions were packed into the ammunition bays of my aircraft, and in the radio compartment behind my seat. I had only just jumped down into the mud when a Bofors gun at the end of the aerodrome fired two rounds. Everyone started to run. Three German bombers appeared out of the cloud with their bomb bays open, and I saw the bombs start to fall.

The slit trenches were about fifty yards away with chaps calling to us. I wasted no time in reaching them and diving in. The first bombs burst right on our dispersal, and my aeroplane received a direct hit. There was little left, and that was the end of my clothing and other gear. Replacements were non-existent just then, but the other pilots helped out with the necessary things. Having lost my aircraft, I wasn't terribly useful, so I was given a sick Spitfire to fly back to Algiers, and from there I travelled by C47 to Gibraltar again to collect another which I flew back to Bône, arriving on 27th November, 1942. So started a very active month or so.

Our Spitfires were a tropicalised version with a large (and ugly) addition under the nose called a Volkes filter. This was required to keep dust and other small objects out of the engine intake. Whilst quite efficient at achieving its purpose, this reduced the performance of the aircraft markedly; by twenty percent some said. Thus our Spitfires were not a match for the ME 109Gs and FW 190s against which we were pitted, and this caused our good health to be very definitely endangered in the ensuing month. This situation made me recall the state of respect and fear in which these German fighters were held by the RAF in Britain when the much more efficient Mk Vs (*sans* Volkes filters) were used on offensive sweeps over France. I wondered just how I would fare.

The pilots of 81 Squadron, when I met them, seemed to me to be a hard-bitten bunch with considerable experience behind them. There were several New Zealanders, Flying Officer Montgomerie, and Sergeants Plummer and Loftus being three of them. We were all billeted in a hotel in the middle of the town of Bône, which was an old seaport and the most forward harbour for the supply shipping serving the 1st Army. The only anti-aircraft defences were some heavy AA guns and a few Bofors, plus of course whatever the shipping in the harbour could put up, which was sometimes quite formidable. Our aerodrome was the erstwhile airport near the town, and this was the base of three Spitfire squadrons; 81, 242, and an American squadron which we dubbed the 'American Pursuit Outfit'. This latter squadron was manned by USAAF regular pilots who were gaining experience prior to taking command of American fighter squadrons. They performed most creditably under the same trying conditions from which we suffered.

At this time bombing went on day and night, together with strafing of our airfield during the day. It was wintertime and the conditions were both cold and wet. We either sat huddled in our shattered dispersal on readiness, or in slit trenches during raids, or strapped in our machines ready for a quick take-off, or up in the air on patrol. During the night we kept to our rooms on the second floor of our commandeered hotel, trying to sleep while bombs roared overhead on their way to the harbour, a short distance away. We seemed to have very few fine, dry, and warm days at that time of the year, and my recollection of our dispersal at the aerodrome is of a cold, damp and draughty place where we sat at readiness on the concrete floor of the old airport passenger terminal, with rain and wind blowing in through gaps which once were windows. There were no chairs, and the daily bombing and strafing attacks saw to it that comfort was absent. Chatting was our only diversion except once when one of our members who shall remain nameless, after cleaning his revolver, reloaded it, cocked it and then pulled the trigger. The bullet ricocheted around the concrete walls and didn't hit a soul. The perpetrator went white with shock. A form of Russian roulette I suppose!

The night raids started at dusk, and continued every few minutes until dawn. With no real night defences, it was like a milk run for the German and Italian bombers. The evening usually started with an air raid warning and the thunder of feet as others rushed downstairs to shelters. After a few such excursions ourselves, we opted to stay where we were, and try to sleep, hoping that the bomb aimers would be accurate and miss us. After about five days of this, the air force command must have decided that the potential loss of all its pilots in one hit wasn't acceptable, and we were told to get out and find other billets. The very next night, the bomb aimers were not so accurate, and our hotel took several direct hits and was destroyed. We were lucky. Perhaps luck isn't quite the correct word, for Nazi sympathisers abounded in the town, and we were fairly certain that our location had been passed on.

It was fend for oneself then, and we, the sergeant pilots, selected an abandoned villa on the seafront just around a headland from the harbour. From there we were out of the line of bomb dropping, and could see everything that went on. Nightly, a grand pyrotechnic display was mounted by attacking air-craft and defensive flak. Helmets were necessary if outside for shrapnel falling from anti-aircraft missiles landed around us like rain for some time after the raid had ceased. I have wondered since how many tons of steel the modern townsfolk must be digging up in their gardens.

The villa was fully furnished, although short of beds, was comfortable, and became the sergeants' mess. We had no rations, no cook, and had to find enough food daily by cadging, thieving, and demanding whatever we could find. The poor chaps on their day off had the job. Some of our fellows turned out to be very able thieves, and not bad cooks. The merchant navy in the harbour was a good source of food, and we received the odd loaf of bread from various ships. To help out we were granted half a case of invasion rations daily, so didn't actually starve, but food sources were short.

A word or two about our own operations. Our main task was to protect the harbour and its shipping, plus to escort whatever convoys were coming in. We had against us Luftwaffe fighters from a base in Tunisia called Bizerta, and bombers from Sicily. Also the Reggia Aeronautica (Italy) sent over the occasional fighter. Some Stukas were also stationed at Bizerta. With no radar or other long-range warning devices available, we were forced to keep a patrol of two Spitfires over the airfield all day to buy time to get the other aircraft off in the event of a raid. In addition, another two were strapped in waiting at the end of the runway for an inevitable scramble. The remainder were at readiness in the dispersal.

German fighter raids were a frequent occurrence, and unescorted bombers sometimes cheekily made an appearance hoping to catch us unawares, such as happened when I arrived to join the squadron. Also on many mornings, and during the day, some keen German fighter ace would do a lone reconnaissance in the hope of chalking up another victory. They usually came in low, and disappeared again rapidly. One of these fellows, one morning, came off the sea at first light and shot down a Hurricane landing behind me. Luckily he was content with just one victim, as I was also vulnerable, just touching down on the runway. Apart from the daily fighting, and the losses which ensued, three particular incidents are still fresh in my mind. As I was new and relatively untried, I wished to get into as much action as I could, but very soon after, I wasn't so keen.

The first incident relates to the Italian Air Force, the Reggia Aeronautica. I was on patrol one morning when I sighted two enemy aircraft, which turned out to be Macchi 202 fighters. Rather precipitately, without seeing his number two, I attacked the leader and was just going to fire my cannons and machine guns at him, when I noticed a lot of tracer passing close to my cockpit. I immediately broke hard to port, and saw my assailant, his number two, diving for the sea with his leader. Both escaped unscathed. It was the number two which nearly shot me down. He did actually hit me in the oil cooler. I was most surprised at the small calibre of his machine guns. The holes were the equivalent of our 22 calibre but of course were a much higher power.

The next episode concerned Italian bombers, which made an unescorted daytime raid on our base on 1st December, but which in fact got nowhere near us. It was a cloudy, damp, but warm morning, and I was sitting strapped into the cockpit of my Spitfire at the end of what we still called a runway (it was much pitted with repaired bomb craters), when my section received an order to scramble. The two of us (I cannot remember the name of my partner) took off and climbed hard under the direction of the controller. He didn't seem to be too sure of what was going on, except that some Spitfires were attacking enemy bombers.

I could hear them talking to each other, and thought that they would assist us to join them. We asked the said Spitfires where they were, using our RT (radio telephony). There was no reply. So we continued climbing on the course set by the controller, and broke through the cloud to see in front of us in the distance four or five bombers being harried by the Spitfires. My number two disappeared at about this time and it transpired that he had had to return to base with oil pressure trouble. I flew at full throttle towards the mêlée (the enemy bombers turned out to be Italian S-84s), and arrived just as they disappeared into the cloud. Cursing my luck, I followed them into the cloud, and descended.

Just as I broke out from the bottom of the cloud there was an enemy bomber right ahead. The idiot had gone below cloud cover. Keeping just in the misty base of the cloud so that he wouldn't see me, I overhauled the bomber and opened fire with cannons and machine guns at point blank range of about fifty yards from dead astern. Great pieces flew off, and the bomber appeared to stop in mid-air, so that I nearly collided with it. The nose went down, and I followed in a near vertical dive, giving it another burst to make sure. I later felt rather bad about the second burst when the bomber was doomed anyway. It crashed into the sea. Then I realised that there was another bomber just ahead of the first, but by then, I had given my presence away. I chased the second bomber at full throttle and caught up. This time his gunners were ready and fire came from the tail and side locations, but missed me. I made an attack but had used up all my cannon ammunition on the first bomber so had only my machine guns. I poured a long burst into the bomber from my four Browning 303s until these ran dry. Smoke was pouring from one engine and vapour of some sort from the other, and I reluctantly had to leave. It was still flying though.

During my attacks there was no sign of any other Spitfires, so it appeared that these had given up the chase. I returned home and claimed one destroyed and one damaged. Much later we heard that eleven bombers had been sent unescorted to bomb us in broad daylight, with a result that ten had been shot down. The survivor had wisely remained in the cloud cover. I believe that my bomber claimed damaged didn't reach home and therefore had become a destroyed aircraft but never credited.

My next combat was in less propitious circumstances. I was on patrol with a flying officer as his number two, when I saw away to port a number of fighters (actually there were twelve of them), which I took to be ME 109s. Being keen, and believing it to be policy to attack at all times, I notified my leader of their presence and went straight into the attack. My leader didn't follow and, perhaps wisely, immediately flew back to base with the firm opinion that I had committed suicide. Indeed, he reported me as having been shot down, and I believe that the usual post mortem activities were actually put in train. Having made my initial attack which damaged one, I immediately found myself in trouble with ME 109s attacking me from all sides. The knowledge that I was more manoeuvrable and behind our own lines was quite comforting, even though I didn't have much chance of survival if the current thinking in Britain when caught on one's own was anything to go by.

Initially I stayed on the same level hoping to turn inside my opponents and get a shot at them, but this bunch had some really experienced and capable pilots, and I soon found myself in dire trouble. I remembered the story told to me by an old First World War mentor and friend, and decided that none of these bastards were going to get me without well and truly earning their victory. So I used my manoeuvrability to keep just under the nose of each attacking ME 109 so that he couldn't get me squarely in his sights. They attacked in pairs; one pair executing an attack on me while another pair situated itself for another attack to follow, and so on ad infinitum with all twelve being involved. I dived under the noses of the first pair, knowing that a second pair was coming down on my tail. I noted the cannons firing from the first pair and sincerely hoped that their salvo would miss, which it did. I then whipped around to dive under the noses of the second pair while other pairs readied themselves for another attack.

As there were twelve ME 109s, it was possible that up to six pairs took part in the attacks, but I was too busy to notice. Altogether, quite a lot of German ammunition was being wasted. The attacks continued and we lost height rapidly as I twisted and turned violently. I was just starting to consider what I should do when altitude ran out, when the attacks were broken off and the German squadron flew off, quite possibly because fuel was running low, or their CO was becoming wary of attacks from other Spitfires.

It occurred to me that the German CO must have had some scathing things to say about his pilots' marksmanship, because apart from my initial opening fire, I had had no chance to use my guns without leaving myself wide open to a burst myself. I saw another lone Spitfire some distance away, and joined him for company. It turned out to be another New Zealander friend, Harry Moore of 242 Squadron. Together we returned to Bône where I wasn't exactly received with open arms. I was immediately put on the mat by my flying officer leader, who gave me a dressing down in front of the other pilots, and sent me to the CO.

While I was feeling rather embarrassed at the fellow's behaviour, it did help to hear another pilot, Flying Officer 'Gus' Large, a Canadian tell him to "tone it down", and say "it is a pity we haven't a few more like him". Gus, together with quite a number of other experienced pilots, was shot down and killed in the next few days. Included were two New Zealanders, Tony Plummer and Sergeant Loftus. Tony and I had been on the same course in New Zealand.

The CO, Squadron Leader Razz Berry, gave me the message that we weren't intended to be a lot of individual 'cowboys', and in future I was to follow my section leader's orders before charging in to the attack. He then dismissed me with a gesture and a big wink. The post mortem activities on my behalf were brought to an abrupt halt and my personal belongings remained intact. Perhaps this observation is a little unfair. When one of our number was killed or missing believed killed, his personal belongings were collected by the adjutant (we didn't rate a padre), and sent off to next of kin. Issued clothing and other gear was shared out among the surviving pilots. That way, we managed to stay reasonably well dressed. A clothing store was the last thing on the minds of squadron administrators under forward operating conditions.

9
Night Flights and Hallucinations

Daily the bitter fighting went on, and daily we lost more pilots, until finally we were worn down to one serviceable Spitfire left from the sixteen we started with, and about ten pilots out of the thirty odd of a full establishment. All this time our airfield and the harbour had been subjected to unceasing day and night strafing and bombing attacks, and the Germans even had the cheek to use outdated Stuka dive-bombers, such was their air superiority. I was on a rest day on that occasion, but watched from a vantage point. The Stukas suffered quite heavy casualties.

Each day our airfield had its new bomb craters filled in by army engineers, and we dodged holes, weak patches and other hazards while taking off and landing. One day I walked to the runway edge to talk to the army officer supervising three men working on patching up a hole as a Spitfire came in to land. What followed was a particularly nasty incident which has been mentioned in one or two books. The men pulled off to the side of the runway and the Spitfire ran into a weak patch while still at speed. This caused it to swerve and its wing took the heads off all three soldiers who had been working on the craters. The lieutenant and I were only a matter of yards from the scene, and both of us were severely shocked. I almost had to physically restrain the officer from attacking the pilot. Both were very upset. This incident has been misreported in several books unfortunately. So far as I know, the lieutenant, myself, and the pilot who is still alive at the time of writing, were the only ones near the incident.

One day at last, a night-fighting Beaufighter arrived from its base at Maison Blanche, to deal with the so far unchallenged night bombing. The intention was that it arrived during the day and scrambled from Bône, and after doing its stuff, would return to Maison Blanche as Bône was no place to land at night. Night flying facilities were primitive to say the least. A row of kerosene tins containing lit hurricane lamps was placed at intervals down the longest usable runway at dusk. The plan was that when the night-fighter was scrambled, the duty pilot for the night would proceed out to the runway and lift flaps in the kerosene tins thus providing the night-fighter pilot with runway lighting. This didn't work very well because a lack of oxygen caused the lights to go out.

I was duty pilot one night on my own when a scramble was ordered, and I drove out in a Jeep to the runway in pitch blackness while the Beaufighter sat with its engines roaring waiting for the runway lights to show. It was raining, and the place was a sea of mud off the runway. I stumbled about trying to find the kerosene tins only to find that most of the hurricane lamps had gone out. I managed to get three alight when the Beaufighter pilot decided he couldn't wait any longer, and started to take off with the benefit of only three lights and his instruments. I dived into the mud and hoped that he would keep straight and not run over me. He got off safely. I found my jeep again in the darkness and repaired to the dispersal as fast as I could go. There, I hopped into the cockpit of a Spitfire and listened in on the RT hoping to hear what was going on.

The controller was vectoring the Beaufighter quite close to the aerodrome, and I could hear his engines as well as those of the enemy bombers. Suddenly the pilot reported that he had the enemy on his radar and was closing for the kill. Shortly after, I saw a burst of cannon fire and an aircraft went down in flames. The night-fighter pilots, with so much unsuspecting trade, soon ran up big scores, and then the bombing stopped while the enemy obviously considered their position. If anything however, the daylight raids intensified, and as mentioned earlier, our squadrons ran out of aeroplanes and pilots.

This was a nerve-wracking period and quite a few pilots suffered nervous breakdowns which manifested themselves in a range of ways from reluctance to get into combat, to irrational behaviour, to physical and mental disturbances, and sometimes to hallucinating. These pilots were rapidly moved away from the squadron environs. Some were given the dreaded title of LMF, lack of moral fibre. Today this is not regarded as something to be ashamed of. All of us were under considerable nervous tension, and like front line soldiers, looked upon the dawn and wondered if we would see another tomorrow. Small things like the sunlight, trees, birds, and other living things assumed an unusual importance, clarity, and value in our limited world, and helped us to keep a sense of what was normal. I suppose it could be called sanity. One felt seriously vulnerable and mortal.

An example of the dangers of hallucination was brought home to me quite forcibly during this period. We had just returned from an operation, and were in the circuit preparing to land when a Spitfire from 242 Squadron flew up behind me in a very aggressive manner, and I suspected he was lining up to shoot me down. He continued with his attack, and I started to take evasive action. At the same time I heard a member of his own squadron ask him what the hell he thought he was doing. He broke off, and I landed determined to ask him the very same question. I was feeling rather angry and aggressive about it, as I didn't at all like the thought of being shot down by one of our own.

After we had all landed, I went to the dispersal of 242 Squadron with the intention of having it out with the culprit. It then transpired that he had been taken off for psychiatric evaluation, having hallucinated that I was an enemy fighter. He was a flight commander and we never saw him again. It is bad enough to have an enemy determined on one's swift demise, without one of your own doing the same thing. But it did happen. Just one of the operational hazards which exist during wartime.

Another rather peculiar incident worried me considerably at the time. Two of us were on a defensive patrol during the period described above, and I must admit that I was suffering some nervous stress. We were flying parallel with one another, and weaving to ensure maximum visibility around us, and to avoid presenting a nice target for any enemy which eluded our vigilance. We were in contact with base through our VHF (very high frequency) radio, which was crystal controlled and could not possibly be used to listen to normal broadcast stations. Suddenly in my earphones I could quite clearly hear a solo harp playing.

Through my interest in classical music, I was quite aware of how a harp sounded, so that there was no error in my recognition of the instrument. Harp solos are exceedingly rare in broadcast music, and I was greatly alarmed. I didn't dare ask my number two whether he could hear it because he would probably report my imminent mental breakdown to the medical officer, who kept an eye on pilots for just this state. I wondered if I was still in the land of the living, if not, death wasn't as bad as I had thought it might be. A hard pinch on the leg convinced me I was still alive. My patrol finished without a combat on this occasion, and I kept quiet about my experience for some days, but it prayed on my mind.

Curiosity forced me eventually to consult our engineering officer who was the fount of all technical knowledge. That 'gentleman' assured me that under no circumstances was it possible to hear a broadcasting station over our VHF radio. Then he must have promptly let his fellow officers know about it, for I received unmerciful ribbing with comments such as "it is an omen", and "your time has come". All of this went on in a jocular manner, but it certainly had me worried at the time. A year later in India, I suddenly heard a dance band playing in my earphones while flying. This time our august engineering officer admitted that it might be possible to hear such things if the atmospheric conditions were right and the broadcast frequency was such that a harmonic of the broadcast frequency perfectly fitted the crystal frequency of my VHF set. So the agony of waiting expectantly for my imminent demise had been quite unnecessary. What is of interest however, is the chance of a freak atmospheric condition occurring simultaneously with the broadcast of a solo harp item. One in many millions I should think. Was there a message in this?

10
A Change of Venue and Aeroplanes

Just as we were wondering what we could do with only one aeroplane, we were relieved. Within a very short time we were on our way in trucks to a town called Constantine deep in the desert country of Algeria. There we spent a restful time recouping our energies. Days were spent in exploring the old Arab streets, purchasing sweetmeats, which were abundant, especially a type of coloured meringue. We also visited the ancient city of Timgad, a sister city of Carthage. There we were given a lot of old Roman coins, some of which I managed to bring home, but have since lost.

One evening we were all celebrating with good Algerian wine when the CO, Razz Berry, who was a little tipsy, jocularly accused me of being a deserter. I pricked up my ears at that, and asked for an explanation. He then told me that when things had settled down after the 'Torch' landings, the squadron adjutant had reported my arrival on the squadron, along with others, and a message had come back to say that I was wanted as a deserter, and the powers-that-be had been looking for me.

Apparently, shortly after I had left Gibraltar with Larry Cronin and Bill Caldecott, I had received a posting but couldn't be found. Razz Berry had said that he wished to keep me on 81 Squadron, and had apparently pulled strings to cancel any punitive action under contemplation. Anyway, nothing further happened, but I expect the Brits had harsh things to say about insubordinate New Zealanders.

We had twenty days rest at Constantine, after which we went to Gibraltar to pick up our new aircraft, Spitfire Mk IXs. These were quite an improvement on our old Mk Vs with two stage superchargers and an entirely new and more powerful Merlin engine of the 61 and 63 series. (The Mk V had a Merlin 47 series). Seven days were spent in getting used to these new aircraft which we expected to prove more than a match for our German opponents.

As part of proving the tropical performance of these new aeroplanes I was sent on a height test over Gibraltar while being tracked by radar. I reached 50,000 feet on my altimeter, and was breathing pure oxygen although unpressurised, when I lost control in the rarefied air and could do nothing with the aeroplane until I reached 20,000 feet again in a pendulum type dive. Recovery was standard and I returned to base at high speed, about 460 mph. The radar tracked me at slightly lower than 50,000 feet, but I prefer to believe my altimeter. At that altitude the sky was inky black, and I could see a long way down the African coast, and up towards Portugal. It was a great view, and all the better as I had time to enjoy it with no enemy aircraft waiting to attack me.

On 28th January, 1943, we returned to a new airstrip near Bône, called Tingley, named after the engineer who built the strip. The surface was lined with interlocking steel sheets which gave it an all-weather capability. Tingley was hidden behind a hill from Bône, and the Germans seemed to be unaware of its existence, so we were spared from the previous bombing and strafing. Attacks still continued on the old airport, which was covered with wrecks of real aircraft, plus some model ones to create the illusion of a busy fighter station. We now had a new commanding officer, Squadron Leader Colin Gray, a New Zealander, who was one of the RAF's leading aces. Razz Berry had been promoted to wing commander of our wing. With our new Spitfire Mk IXs we went on the offensive, and patrolled at squadron strength well behind the enemy lines.

The Germans seemed to be having a rest also, because things were fairly quiet except for anti-aircraft fire. Because we were manoeuvrable we did not worry too much about the AA fire, and rather enjoyed the cat and mouse game of out-guessing the German gunners. They soon tired of wasting good ammunition however, and would not open up a barrage unless they were firing at bombers. We did quite a few bomber escorts at this time, and were successful at keeping the enemy fighters at bay. The bombers did however, have to face very heavy and accurate AA fire, especially as they made their run up to the target. On such occasions we would move to one side, out of harm's way. Sounds miserable in retrospect. It wasn't until March that we had fighter reaction to our taunting sweeps, and then daily we

had combats, this time with more success and fewer
losses.

While at Tingley my new aeroplane kept having
engine failure. The problem was intermittent and
hard to trace. The failure usually occurred at critical
times such as take-off or when in combat, or when
landing and a burst of power was required. All
power was suddenly lost, but the engine would still
idle with just enough power to stay in the air.
Rather embarrassing and decidedly dangerous
when jousting with the enemy, and I had to break
off combat precipitously twice, while sincerely
hoping that my opponent didn't realise the reason.

Each time the engine fitters investigated and
could find nothing wrong. After the group captain,
Peter Hugo, had borrowed my aircraft for a sortie,
and had nearly killed himself on take-off when the
engine failed again, the fuel system was completely
dismantled, and a spark plug cap was discovered in
the main supply line leading to the carburettor. This
moved when the flow for full power was applied,
and blocked the entry to the carburettor. When the
flow ceased through lack of power after the
blockage, the cap fell back and allowed some sort of
flow to occur thus permitting the aeroplane to stay
in the air. Was this sabotage or carelessness at the
assembly works?

It was unusual for our ground crew to be careless
or to make mistakes, and there were strict
procedures to be followed to prevent this. Nevertheless, on another occasion a careless mistake was
made which nearly cost me my life. Sometimes it
was necessary to remove the pilot's seat from the
aircraft. The seat was a heavy unit with armour

plate attached down the back and underneath, to protect the pilot from shells and bullets fired from behind. The bottom of the seat was located in position by two lugs which fitted into slots to provide a fulcrum on which the whole seat pivoted. The seat was locked into its proper position at the top rear by two sliding pins which locked behind the pilot. Should these pins not be properly located, the whole seat could rotate forwards and downwards, thus jamming the controls which ran under the seat. Interference with the controls caused by such jamming could have serious consequences.

On this occasion, having removed and replaced the pilot's seat, my crew failed to lock the rear pins properly in place. While involved in a combat with some ME 109s my seat suddenly slumped forward and jammed my elevator controls. I was in a fast dive at the time and none of the enemy followed me down. I had aileron and rudder control, but the elevators were immovable, and I had to recover from the dive quickly. Wrenching at the control column had no effect, but in desperation I found that by putting my feet on the instrument panel and pushing back hard, I lifted the seat sufficiently to allow some use of the elevators. I managed to change the dive to a climb, but was jammed into that. With some trouble I neutralised the elevators, and by use of the trimming tabs I could change attitude in the pitching plane.

Landing was the next problem and this would have to be made without the use of flaps because of the sudden change of attitude in the pitching plane when the flaps were lowered. A much longer landing run could be expected. I managed to land successfully with the use of trim tabs in the early stages and by the use of feet on the instrument panel and brute strength on the control column to flare out and to keep the aeroplane from lifting into the air again in the final stages. I was very lucky to get down without crashing or damaging the aircraft. No doubt other pilots had encountered similar problems but I hadn't heard of any, and with two incidents in quick succession, I felt that I was receiving more than my fair share.

Carelessness on the part of ground crews was rare, but it did occur, especially when the ground crew were under pressure from lack of sleep and fatigue. I wonder how many pilots lost their lives through this type of incident? Much later, I again very nearly lost mine through another similar type of carelessness.

On 1st March we moved to a more forward strip called Paddington, near Souk el Khemis, and made this our base. It was a pleasure getting away from Tingley with its chilly and hostile atmosphere. To me it was a place with bad memories. Life was spartan, and our mess was a hole in the ground on the airstrip itself. The digging of the hole with Squad-ron Leader Gray wielding a shovel while we watched his example, was photographed by Cecil Beaton, and appeared in a copy of the *London Illustrated News* some time later (a copy of this photograph is on display at the Wanaka fighter pilot's museum). Our first task at Paddington was to dig slit trenches for shelter from bombing and strafing, and to get our mess established in its own hole. Our sleeping quarters were in scattered tents located in another valley some distance away.

The countryside was dry and bare of trees, and it was quite hot. A sparse covering of long withered grass was the only growth that I remember. This was the home of a number of venomous snakes, including the black and green mambas, and very big and poisonous centipedes. There were also scorpions. Indeed there were more snakes around our quarters than I saw at any time elsewhere in our travels. Someone had a joke at our expense one day by placing a dead green mamba nicely posed on the path leading to our tent. I don't know who suffered from a heart attack when he came upon it during the night but it wasn't me. Water was short and we were strictly rationed.

One night we had retired to our tent, which accommodated four men, and the tent was tightly laced to avoid showing light. A pilot called 'Major' Brown was in bed on his camp stretcher holding forth quite volubly on some subject, when he suddenly seemed to levitate, and he somehow shot through the tent wall to end up outside. We were very surprised and most intrigued until he told us that a snake was crawling up his belly. A general and hurried exodus ensued, and then there was an argument as to who would go in to deal with the snake. I forget who the brave person was, but he went in with drawn revolver and found that the said snake was a foot long centipede. It was fortunate that Major wasn't bitten. I didn't ever hear of anyone being bitten, but I am sure that some must have been.

The said Major was not impressed with what he called the New Zealander's agricultural accent. He insisted on taking me under his wing to improve my pronunciation. A typical example would be to break into my conversation should I for instance be speaking about sharks, to admonish "the pronunciation is not 'shack', but 'shaak'". I just cannot get the phonetics right. He was a good friend and comrade who later had a terrible crash from which he suffered a permanent dent in his skull, but he returned and flew with us again. I don't know what eventually happened to him; like so many he just disappeared.

Above: Hawker Hinds at Ohakea RNZAF Station, 1941.

Left: First flight. What are we in for? Bell Block, New Plymouth, 1941. LACs Trafford and Peart.

FLIGHT 2B
SQUADRON 1.
Levin

Above: Our flight at ITW, Levin, 1941 (author 2nd from left, front row).

Right: Alan Peart and Joel Treister in the cockpit of a Hawker Hind, Levin. Note the gun machine port.

Top: Hawker Hind and trainee pilots, RNZAF, 1941. LAC Alan Peart leaning against propeller.

Bottom left: LAC Alan Peart with new brevet, 1941.

Bottom right: Sergeant Pilot Alan Peart on final leave, 1941.

Top: Course 16. New Zealand fighter pilots in training at RAF Hullavington, UK.

Middle: The author in the cockpit of his first Hurricane. RAF Hullavington, UK.

Bottom: Pilots of 610 Squadron, 1942. Squadron Leader 'Johnnie' Johnson with his dog at front centre. Sergeant Alan Peart is in the back row, fifth from right.

Top: Squadron Leader 'Razz' Berry, 81 Squadron, at Bône, North Africa, 1942.

Middle left: Alan Peart and 'Chubby' Husband at Tingley, North Africa.

Middle right: Spitfire Mk 9, 81 Squadron, RAF Tingley.

Bottom: Ground crew and pilots from 81 Squadron at Tingley. Alan Peart in Vichy cap and Syd Moston in fez.

Top: Morning ablutions at Tingley.
Middle: FW190, the opposition! Bizerta, North Africa, 1943.
Bottom: Remains of a Ju52 troop carrier, Luftwaffe, Bizerta.

Top: ME109G of JG53 (the ace of spades) at Bizerta.

Middle: FW190, Bizerta.

Bottom: ME109G of JG53 after delousing, Bizerta.

Top left: Crashed FW190, Bizerta, 1943.

Top right: Sergeant Pilot Harry Moore, 242 Squadron RAF, on rest at Constantine, North Africa.

Bottom: 81 Squadron pilots on rest at Constantine. Left to right: Sergeant Pilots Irvine (UK), Peart (NZ), Cronin (AUS), Robinson (NZ), Pilot Officer Peppler (CAN), Sergeant Pilot Hamelin (CAN).

Top: Sergeant Pilot 'Major' Brown far right with an FW190.

Middle: What's Up? 81 Squadron, Paddington, North Africa. 1943. Left to right: Flying Officer Montgomerie (NZ), Flight Lieutenant Bill Goby (UK), Flight Lieutenant Harry Byford (UK), Flying Officer Peppler (CAN).

Bottom: Squadron Leader Colin Gray (NZ). 81 Squadron, RAF Paddington, North Africa, 1943.

Top: One of ours! The results of a prang.

Middle: Pilots and ground crew, RAF Paddington, North Africa. Left to right: back row – 'Chiefy' Saxton, Flying Officer Bill Fell (CAN), Sergeant Pilot 'Major' Brown (UK), Sergeant Pilot Colin Campbell (UK), Sergeant Burton, Sergeant Pilot Graham Hulse (UK), Flying Officer Montgomerie (NZ). Front Row: Sergeant Pilot Don Rathwell (CAN), Squadron Leader Colin Gray (NZ), Flight Lieutenant Bill Goby (UK).

Bottom: NCI pilots, outside our tents at Paddington. Bill Hayes far left, Alan Peart second from left, Bill Caldecott fourth from right, Larry Cronin third from right.

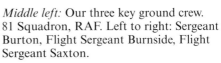

Middle left: Our three key ground crew. 81 Squadron, RAF. Left to right: Sergeant Burton, Flight Sergeant Burnside, Flight Sergeant Saxton.

Middle right: Civilian escape photograph taken in Malta. A bad fit in jackets.

Bottom left: Flying Officer Larry Cronin with commandeered car. Goia, Italy.

Bottom right: The Four Musketeers. Left to right: Sergeant Pilots Jim Robinson, Alan Peart, Bill Caldecott and Larry Cronin.

Top left: Our dispersal, mess and social centre on the airstrip, Paddington, North Africa.

Top right: A very rare bath. Paddington, North Africa.

Top: Damaged Spitfire Mk 9 after night bombing raid. 81 Squadron, Lentini, Sicily, 1943.

Bottom: Macchi C202 Fighter, Italian Air Force, Lentini, Sicily. Flown by 81 Squadron pilots.

Top left: Pilot Officer Alan Peart, Cairo, 1943.
Top right: Pilot Officer Alan Peart and Flight Sergeant Pat Ryan, Calcutta, 1943.

Bottom: Pilots and ground crew, 81 Squadron, Kanglatombi, Imphal Valley, 1944.

Top: Our quarters after a monsoon storm. Khumbhirgram, Assam, India, 1944.

Middle left: Larry Cronin with his ground crew. 81 Squadron, India, 1944.

Middle right: Taking the sun! Peart and Cronin, Kanglatombi.

Bottom: Flying Officer Peart with a Spitfire Mk 8, 1944.

Top: 81 Squadron pilots with Spitfire Mk 8, Minnerya, Ceylon.

Middle: August 1944, Ceylon. Author kneeling in centre.

Bottom: Instructors at the fighter training unit, Poona, India, 1944. Flight Lieutenant Alan Peart fourth from right, back row.

Top: ANZAC Day parade, 1946.

Bottom left: RNZAF Identification card.

Bottom right: The ancient and the modern. Alan Peart with his niece Squadron Leader Heather Peart, RNZAF. ANZAC Day, 25th April, 2007.

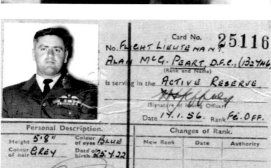

11
Combat, Air Raids and Rest

Anzac Day, 25th April 1943, turned out to be a day to remember. Two days earlier I had damaged an ME 109G but today I was with an offensive patrol when we were attacked by a number of ME 109s which flew through us in a diving head on attack. We took evasive action, and in the ensuing mêlée I latched onto a ME 109 which climbed hard with me hot on his tail. He either didn't know I was there or he thought he could out perform me, because he just kept climbing and turning ahead of me. I put in one burst with cannons and machine guns, which hit him, but didn't seem to do any discernable serious damage. Just as I was ready to fire again, his canopy flew off and the pilot baled out, his body just missing my wing. We were well split up by then, and I returned to base to find that my number two was missing. He must have been hit in the first attack, and I didn't see it. I felt very badly about that as a leader is supposed to look after his number two, who is usually an inexperienced pilot. He was the first I had lost, and I felt responsible. This was a busy period for the Luftwaffe and of course us, and the squadron was involved in continuous scrambles and fighter operations.

On one of my days off, with no flying scheduled and nothing to do, I spent the day at the dispersal with the rest of the pilots who were on duty. Just not having to fly was as good as a rest at that time. The squadron was just taking off on an operation when two warning shots from a Bofors AA gun were fired. This signalled an imminent air raid. Such warnings were frequent, but many were false alarms, so I wasn't particularly perturbed about this one. One of our ground crew was a New Zealand corporal who had been decorated with the BEM for some meritorious action in the past, and this chap ran past me obviously aiming for cover. As we had had trouble while at Bône with the ground crew running for cover and leaving the pilots strapped in their aircraft still attached to starter batteries while bombs were falling, I didn't want the same thing happening with the squadron in the act of leaving. So I stopped him and suggested that he might not be a good example to other ground crew. Suddenly there was a roar followed immediately by explosions, and not having any time to reach slit trenches, I flung myself flat on the open ground. We were being strafed.

A great cloud of dust rose around me and explosions went past on either side. Six Focke-Wulf 190s had come down out of the sun, and had bounced us. They had strafed our mess area and ground facilities but strangely had left the machines taking off alone. I had been straddled by one burst of fire, which had gone either side without hitting me. I looked for Tomlinson, the name of the corporal, but couldn't see him. He appeared from a ditch about fifty yards away. To this day I have no idea how he covered that distance without being killed. He must have flown. There were many other instances of this type, and perhaps the above can be taken as a typical example. In effect, our ground crew was just as much exposed to enemy bombing and fire as many soldiers, but our ground crew and that of other forward squadrons, perhaps were atypical.

We had disregarded the German breakthrough at Kasserine Pass in Algeria when we were suddenly given orders to ready ourselves for a rapid evacuation in retreat because of the posibility of our being cut off. This came to naught because in the meantime the 1st and 8th Armies were advancing slowly, and we gradually got command of the air, so that the German fighter opposition later almost disappeared. Ultimately, the Afrika Corps and the German army became squeezed into the Cape Bon area, but the presence of some surviving Tiger tanks was causing concern to the Allies. These potent attacking weapons had to be located. Two Spitfires of a reconnaissance squadron were detailed to search the forward areas, and six of us were given the task of providing covering protection. It was all low level, to avoid detection, and our flight took off and flew at about 5,000 feet altitude while the two reconnaissance Spitfires were at a lower altitude.

All was quiet until the two reconnoitring aircraft discovered the tanks and reported their position. Immediately what seemed like hundreds, if not thousands of light anti-aircraft guns opened up in an attempt to stop us returning. These were four barrelled 20 mm Bredas we thought. We had about thirty to forty miles to fly back to our lines and streams of fire like hoses came at us the whole way. I began to understand what a Japanese Kamikaze pilot must have encountered. We jinked around, using all the tricks we knew while streams of shells passed by on both sides of each aircraft as well as behind and ahead. There were enough gunners to pick on individual aircraft, and I remember streams of shells chasing me from side to side as I moved around.

After about five long minutes of dodging we reached our lines, and it was then that Larry Cronin announced that he had been hit and wounded. He received much encouragement and advice, and was allowed to land first before he passed out. His machine had certainly been badly hit, and a shell had passed through the cockpit and his trouser leg on the way. The knock had convinced him that he was wounded. He was unmarked, but he claimed that he could feel the blood running down his leg. A close call for him.

Often after returning from a sortie when a combat or some other traumatic incident had occurred requiring violent action, we found our clothing ripped and scratches on our arms. The movement of our bodies in combat must have been much more violent than we imagined, and our limbs must have come into contact with various projections in the cockpit in spite of being tightly strapped in by a Sutton harness.

Apart from the usual daily sorties and some combats, the North African campaign was nearly over, and we took to strafing troops and trucks etc., bottled up in the Cape Bon area. The Luftwaffe appeared to have gone, and our strafing must have been murderous. Any ships trying to evacuate the German armies were intercepted by the Royal Navy lying in wait just over the horizon at sea. We could hear their big guns at night, and could see the flashes. A hospital ship was tied up to a jetty, and two of us flew down low at high speed to see if there were any German nurses on deck. There were none and no fire came from the ship, so it was left alone. No doubt it was duly checked out by the navy. I couldn't help but feel sorry for the German soldiers bottled up out in the open on the Cape Bon peninsular. Our cannon fire was relentless and there was no escape for the unfortunate soldiers we fired at. It was a very uncomfortable aspect of our work, but war required it.

The campaign finished with the capitulation of the German forces, and there was a great victory parade in Tunis, over which we were given the honour of providing protective cover in case the Germans tried to bomb the VIPs who attended. We finished up based on a field covered with daisies, a beautiful sight after the dry and withered vistas which had been our lot for so long. There we set up camp and slept on the ground in tents. Our days were spent exploring our surroundings, swimming, or testing captured enemy rifles and machine guns of which there was a great assortment lying around. We also visited enemy airfields to get a close view of crashed ME 109s and Focke-Wulf 190s, our erstwhile opponents. One night I woke up feeling very ill with a high temperature, and the rigors. I was also having to make frequent visits to the latrines. Our medico diagnosed dysentery, and I was taken to a casualty clearing station by stretcher. From there I was evacuated by ambulance through other CCSs to a field hospital, some hundreds of miles back it seemed, although I have no real idea. I do remember being attended to by German prisoners of war at one CCS, where they gave me water and a cigarette. They were most careful in handling my stretcher, possibly a sign of mutual respect for each other.

I ended up in a tented hospital where I lay on a stretcher in a ward for several days without treatment of any kind. There was only one overworked nursing sister, and I presume that the medical staff were very busy dealing with the seriously wounded. It was hot. Finally I became restive and decided to leave. I asked for my clothes and was given them. I remember going before a board of three doctors who asked if I had recovered. No medical examination. I assured them that I had, and I was duly released. I wended my way back to the squadron and was welcomed. I suffered from dysentery for months afterwards it seemed, and sometimes regretted my premature action in leaving the hospital without treatment

It was during this period that we discovered that, unlike all other RAF fighter squadrons, 81 Squadron had no official badge, so we decided to design one. Three or four of us got our heads together and contrived a design to fit its known history in the Second World War. I cannot remember the heraldic terms for what we did, but the design incorporated the red star of Russia representing the squadron's period in Russia using Hurricanes under Wing Commander Ramsbottom-

Isherwood (a New Zealander by the way), with a rampant sword which was the emblem of the 1st Army in North Africa. One of our Latin scholars (we had some very erudite fellows as pilots) developed the motto in Latin, and we submitted the lot through the correct channels for approval. To our great surprise and delight the crest and motto were formally approved by the King, and 81 Squadron acquired its formal coat of arms which is still in use today. I feel quite chuffed at the thought that I played a part, however small, in developing the badge of one of the squadrons of the RAF.

Additional to the above, one of the main Luftwaffe units which gave us a hard time in the early stages of the North African campaign was the Richthofen wing JG 53. Its ME 109s sported an ace of spades symbol on the nose of each aeroplane, and the pilots were known as the 'Pik As' boys. Many were the combats we had against them, and we felt that we had eventually triumphed, so what better than to take over their badge. From then on our aeroplanes sported the ace of spades, and we became known as the Ace of Spades Squadron. To cap it off we painted our propeller spinners red, in contravention of orders to have them in duck egg blue, and got away with it. At least we were not ordered to change the colour, and we retained it as our distinctive mark through all the operations which followed, until the end of the war.

I believe that 81 Squadron still retains the ace of spades emblem in peacetime, but the last time I saw an aircraft of 81 Squadron, a Canberra visiting New Zealand, it had an ordinary playing card depicting the ace of spades rather than just the symbol. Perhaps the Germans had exerted pressure to have their emblem protected, and the powers-that-be had given way. Whatever, they could have consulted the old pilots who had at such cost earned the right to that emblem. C'est la guerre I suppose.

When we had moved to Paddington I had been a sergeant pilot for nearly two years without promotion, and a few of us in the same position were not amused to see new pilots joining the Squadron as replacements with the rank of flight sergeant. When we joined the RNZAF, the establishment of NCO ranks was based on a percentage of the total force, and one had to wait for casualties to drop the current percentage before one could get promotion. I think that twenty-five percent of NCOs could be flight sergeants, and ten percent warrant officers. Apparently that had all changed such that a sergeant pilot became a flight sergeant after six months, and a warrant officer after two years. People like myself had been forgotten.

Someone must have lodged a protest because I was suddenly given flight sergeant's rank but backdated only six months, which meant that I had served well over a year as a sergeant. Indeed I was very nearly due for a warrant rank. Apart from the pay considerations, there were other problems. With some squadrons the distinction between officers and NCO pilots became most marked, and in our case it did not please us to have fly as a number two to inexperienced officers, just because we were NCOs. Besides, it was definitely dangerous. The situation apparently had not escaped the attention of our old CO, Wing

Commander Berry, and he arranged for some of us to be recommended for a commission. A Sergeant Rathwell and I were the first to receive commissions, rather late in the piece we both thought.

Leave was infrequent, but special provisions for short rests were made, and I had a total of three of these during the whole of my operational service. The rest centres were usually located in some attractive resort area, and usually a wide range of facilities was available. I had one rest in North Africa, one in Sicily at a place called Taormina, and one in Calcutta in India. There we could sleep in as long as we liked, or could laze about and swim. At Taormina we could sail small dinghies. Earlier in Algeria, and later at Taormina, we encountered the advanced social attitudes practiced by Europeans. This was a shock for backward youths from the deep south. At Constantine young women walked past us without turning a hair as we relieved ourselves at the public urinal, and at Taormina we encountered our first beautiful naked female. She came down to the beach to swim, and ignored our dumbfounded gaze.

After three days of complete relaxation we were sent back to our squadron. I had one leave only, which was given to me while at Tingley in North Africa. Sergeant Pilot Jim Robinson, a New Zealander, accompanied me. We went to Casablanca in French Morocco, where we received wonderful hospitality from the local British and European community. Our leave was for two weeks, but because of transport difficulties we found it most difficult to get back to our Squadron, and it took us overall about four weeks away. Upon our return we found that we were the first of the three pairs given leave to get back. No repercussions. The squadron, after a prolonged rest, then proceeded to Malta.

12
Malta

Upon receiving our direction to Malta, we packed up our meagre belongings, left our daisy field, and flew on a course for the island of Malta. On the way, we passed close to the island of Pantellaria, which was still held by the Italians, but not worth much attention apparently. Later, a pilot happened to land there, and the garrison surrendered to him. Malta was quite hard to see in the permanent haze which seemed to cloud the skies. The island is only about a hundred or so feet above sea level, and easily missed. I wondered how many pilots had overshot it on their way back from Sicily, and had ditched in the sea out of fuel. We landed at a strip called Ta Kali, and each aeroplane, as it landed, was pushed into a blast bay, surrounded by sandbags and protected against bombs. We were quickly brought to readiness, and I had the impression that the people were pleased to see us. The civilian population seemed to be suffering from malnutrition, were thin and had sores. Our food was noticeably meagre but adequate and wholesome.

Action started almost immediately, and dogfights with enemy fighters occurred over Malta daily. Gradually these dwindled in number, and we assumed a more aggressive role by flying to Sicily where the enemy fighters appeared in abundance. Razz Berry was transferred at this time, presumably back to Britain. He was tired and appeared to be suffering badly from strain, so certainly had earned his rest. His place was taken by Colin Gray, who became wing commander, and we received a new CO, a Squadron Leader 'Babe' Whitamore. He was only a day older than myself.

One day, Gray took me as his number two and the pair of us went over to Sicily, where we ran into a large number of ME 109s, and were lucky to catch them unawares, called 'bouncing'. Gray shot one down, and I fired at one but missed. It was my job to protect my number one in an attack, so I was a little distracted. Had I been able to concentrate on my target the result might have been different. Our attack had the effect of stirring up a nest of hornets. We dived for the ground with a horde of ME 109s after us. With throttles fully open and hugging close to the sea as we crossed the Sicilian coast, we headed back to Malta. The following swarm of fighters was just out of range, but this didn't deter them from firing at us when they considered themselves sufficiently close. Every now and then, the sea behind and around us was churned up by cannon shells and bullets. Malta loomed up in the haze in due course, with the ME 109s still keeping us company, and I was starting to consider leading them over our light flak when they turned for home and we could relax. Gray was disappointed that I didn't get one.

As in North Africa, the RAF gradually achieved command of the air, and nearly all sorties were occurring over Sicily. The squadron was no longer equipped entirely with Spitfire Mk IXs. Because there was a shortage of these aircraft we had to share them with other squadrons. So half of the squadron consisted of the Mk IXs while the other half were Spitfire Mk Vs, the same machine which had been so seriously outclassed at Bône. Our squadron formation had to adjust and the Spitfire Mk Vs flew at lower altitudes with the better performing Spitfire Mk IXs above.

On one occasion we were flying with four Mk Vs at a lower altitude, another four slightly higher, and four Mk IXs acting as top cover. The Mk Vs were supposed to watch the rear of the top cover against attack from the sun, while we as top cover kept a close eye on those below, or that was what was supposed to happen. We had discussed the relative responsibilities, and no one should have been in any doubt as to his duties. I was leading a section of the Mk IXs above and relying on the eyes of the lower aircraft to protect my tail, when a ME 109 flew right past me on the same level, having attacked me without being seen by any of the others. I can still see the helmeted and masked enemy pilot staring at me as he passed and then climbed away. He got what we described as the perfect bounce, and I should have been dead. He could not have been a very good shot, or he was distracted from his concentration, because he missed. It should never have happened, and I was furious.

The other section leader climbed hard after the ME 109, which had traded his speed for altitude and fired at him with a difficult nintey degree deflection shot. The burst caught my assailant right in the cockpit, and he was destroyed instead of me. The other section leader was Flying Officer McGuire from Rhodesia, and he made quite a name for himself later with his claims. I resolved never again to trust another with my life or personal safety, and never did. I am afraid that very few had the keen eyesight essential to being a good fighter pilot, and I could hardly blame the others I suppose. I was blessed with superb eyesight and could usually pick up enemy aircraft well before others. A month went by with a lot of air activity, and the invasion of Sicily came about on 10th July.

We patrolled the invasion convoy from dawn to dusk in very bad weather the day before the landing. I had never seen so many ships together at one time. It was said that there were two thousand of them, of all sizes from landing craft to liners with warships spread around them. They were contending with heavy seas, and I wondered how the troops must have been feeling, cooped up below decks as they were. The landing took place early the next morning and was a fiasco because of the stormy weather. Fortunately there was little or no opposition, and the seasick troops got ashore with minimum casualties. In the high winds and bad visibility, other special forces were not so fortunate, airborne troops were dropped in the wrong areas, including the sea, and casualties were heavy. The same applied to glider borne troops. Some of these were released out at sea. Those who were rescued and taken to Malta blamed the air force and went looking for redress. We were confined to barracks until things quietened down.

Our patrols over the invasion fleet now stationary

near the beaches continued, starting before dawn and continuing all day until after dark. My criticism of the navy for its poor aircraft recognition was amply borne out, and thousands of British and American artillery rounds were pumped at us from the ships during this period. We saw no enemy aircraft the whole time, and if any did come near the fleet there weren't many. At times the 'friendly' fire came uncomfortably close, and we were not amused. The American and British armies advanced into Sicily and Malta became too remote as a fighter base. We moved to a forward airfield in Sicily.

13
Sicily

On 19th July, 1943, we left Malta and flew to a new base, a pair of airstrips called the Lentini satellites just south of Catania, and inland from Augusta. We had a strip to share with another squadron while others used the adjacent strip. As these two strips were at right angles to each other, an arrangement had to be made for squadrons using one strip to keep low on take-off while those using the other strip were to climb steeply after take-off, so avoiding mid-air collisions. Overlooking our strip was a hill upon which we established our mess and sleeping quarters.

Much of our work was now escorting bombers on raids and carrying out offensive patrols. Contacts with enemy fighters were beginning to taper off now that we had command of the air. However, the enemy anti-aircraft fire was proving to be voluminous and accurate. This was because of the large number of AA guns cooped up in a fairly small space in Sicily. These were closely grouped around tactical targets which our forces wished to attack. I received hits from this for the first time, and on a number of occasions was blown onto my back by close bursts. My tail wheel burst once from a close explosion. The greatest danger was when providing close escort to bombers.

It was summertime, and Sicily proved to be very dry and very hot. Grape harvesting was going on, and the local people pressed the grapes for wine by tramping on them in a big vat. I observed the 'trampers' going home to lunch bare-footed along the dusty tracks with their legs red with grape juice. They then returned and jumped straight into the vats. Perhaps the dust, germs, and heaven knows what else, mixed in with the grape juice, give the Sicilian wine its renowned flavour.

Our few hours of leisure were spent immersing ourselves in the local swampy creek to keep cool. One of our number, 'Moon' Collingwood, a South African captain was sitting in the cool water up to his neck when a water snake (there were quite a few of them) swam inquisitively up behind him and peered at his neck. We asked Moon to look around and were exquisitely amused to observe the pair come face to face at a few inches range. I don't know who got the bigger fright, Moon or the snake. Moon levitated out of the water, and the snake just disappeared. We were told that they were not poisonous, but they were certainly inquisitive.

One day we had a visitor. This was a rare occasion which called for a party. While we were not overburdened with a variety of alcoholic liquors, we always seemed to rustle up something to welcome a guest. He was on this occasion a squadron leader on his way to take command of one of the RAF squadrons in Sicily. At least that is what we understood. He could very well have been just lost and had landed on our strip. He was a nice jolly sort of man who seemed prepared to fit in well and enjoy his stay for the night. He had to accept whatever facilities were available, which sad to say weren't much. Most of us slept on camp beds in tents scattered around a hillside handy to the airstrip.

To digress for a moment, two of our number had chosen to live in a dilapidated building nearby which had attracted their attention. It gave them an interesting night! They were forced to abandon it in the early hours of the morning. They had set up their stretchers inside, made up their camp beds, and climbed in to settle down for a comfortable rest. As soon as it became dark a clanking and rustling sound as of many things moving was heard.

They thought at first a rat might have been responsible. Then one suggested that it might be something haunting the building, particularly as it was a foreign country and one never knew what strange things might have happened there in the past. They decided to take no notice. Anyway, as the night advanced the noise didn't stop, and one of the chaps suddenly sat up complaining that a large thing like a many-legged mouse had run over his face. Both fumbled around for a candle (they didn't have the luxury of a torch) and when it was lit, they saw in the dim light that the whole inside of the building was black with the biggest cockroaches they had ever seen. According to one they clanked like tanks and hissed. The two intrepid campers left in great haste and spent a miserable damp night outside. It made a wonderful breakfast story for the rest of us and caused much merriment. It was noticeable that no-one went to investigate, and so far as I know no attempt was made to use the building again.

After the party which went off well, our visitor was shown to the only bed available, that of an Australian officer who was away on leave. The next morning when we arrived for breakfast quite a rumpus was in progress. Our visitor was there naked to the waste demanding that something be done about an infestation he had encountered in his bed. In the middle of his chest we could see a blue-black berry the size of a small grape. It had legs and was firmly attached to its host. It could only be a fine example of a Sicilian tick.

The most efficient way a tick can be removed with minimal damage to the host is to insert the point of a knife into the flesh beneath the tick's biting head, and to lever the body out, head and all. The resulting small wound can then be disinfected and should heal without further trouble. Our visitor, after some protest, agreed to the recommended procedure. A pocket-knife was produced and the tick was dug out, not without some grunting from the sufferer who was nevertheless quite a stoic. The small wound was swabbed with iodine and a patch put over it. Injured feelings were appeased and the episode was considered closed.

To our surprise the Australian officer who had returned unexpectedly from his leave enquired what all the fuss was about. Upon being told that a tick had been in his bed he immediately accused our overnight guest with bringing vermin into his quarters. Much to our amusement he did this very firmly in the best Australian vernacular. Our visitor took umbrage at the accusation and the whole row erupted anew. However before things became serious the CO intervened and the matter closed with muted muttering continuing from both sides. Our visitor departed later in the morning no doubt swearing never to come near us again. The whole episode was extremely funny although our Australian colleague probably didn't agree. It and the cockroach experience created diversions which were very important in providing us with opportunities to indulge in fun. We had little else in the way of relaxation at that time.

My twenty-first birthday was coming up, and Whitamore, our CO being one day older, decided to toss to determine which day the celebrations were to be held. He of course won, and the party was due on 24th July. The great day dawned, and after the usual daytime activities we had just started to enjoy the party that evening when a flare over our airstrip turned night into day. More followed, and it became apparent that we were due for an air raid. Whitamore ordered all pilots down to the strip, and we all piled into our transport. Down the hillside we went in the light of many flares, and drew up at our dispersal. In the short time we had been at Lentini, we had excavated a large but shallow hole in iron hard earth to provide us with some cover in the event of an air raid. This hole was covered by a tent. Nearby we had also dug a partially completed, shallow slit trench capable of taking two crouched men at a pinch. Neither really gave much protection.

Our aircraft were dispersed all around. We climbed out of our transport just in time to hear the peculiar rushing whistle of bombs coming down. I dived to the ground as a crackle of giant fire works broke out all around. The earth also quaked with heavier explosions. I was lifted off the ground. Someone next to me was shredded, so I thought that I had better find a hole quickly. It was as light as day with the flares, and I flung myself into the sunken dispersal. While in mid-air, I saw a mass of thrashing legs, and I landed right on a pair of feet which kicked heartily, and I found myself outside again. Then I remembered the slit trench we had partially dug. I found it empty and dived in. Meanwhile more HE (heavy explosive) and anti-personnel bombs were falling, and everything seemed to be in flames. The protection to my body provided by the slit trench was most comforting, and I thought sadly of the chap next to me when the first lot of bombs arrived. It was only a few yards away but I couldn't see anybody. Then someone dived in on top of me.

The feeling of a cover over my back was welcome. Then a third chap joined us, and immediately complained that his backside was showing above the ground surface. Could we get lower? We couldn't. I felt perfectly safe with two bodies on top of me, and I certainly could not go any lower. Next, the topmost fellow slid down the side of the trench and squirmed his way under me in spite of my strenuous efforts to stop it. Then I was second. The chap above me started to complain, and did exactly the same thing. I was on top now, and could vouch that protection was indeed extremely limited. I was also not amused, as I had got there first. I did the same thing and fought my way under the bottom chap.

So, with much swearing and cursing at each other, we changed places I don't know how many times while the bombing was going on. When this ceased, we counted the damage. We had no aeroplanes left; all had been destroyed or made unflyable, and we had no transport plus one death, the guy next to me. One of the chaps in the slit trench with me had lost a finger, which he said he had been using to stem the flow of petrol from a tanker. The place looked like Dante's Inferno, with rising columns of smoke and dust illuminated by the flares, burning aircraft, exploding ammunition, and AA guns firing. With Whitamore, I went up the strip to gauge the extent of the damage when above us came the sound of a diving aircraft.

We had been caught out in the open and looked around desperately for some hole or fold in the ground in which to take shelter. There were none. The only thing available was a slit in the hard ground made by a bomb, and not enough to shelter a person. Whitamore saw it first and dived into it. My only recourse was to try to repeat the slit trench trick. I jumped as high as I could and landed hard on Whitamore's back but only managed to force him down about six inches, which wasn't enough cover by far. The aircraft roared over without dropping bombs so was probably one of our night fighters. There was not much we could do until daylight, so we returned to our hilltop campsite and continued our party. So ended our birthday celebrations. I became twenty-one years old the next day.

In daylight the next day we inspected the scene and discovered that not only our squadron but also all of the others (four in total, I think) had been wiped out. The raid was most successful from the German point of view. I received a shock to learn that an unexploded anti-personnel bomb had been found embedded in the corner of the slit trench that we had occupied. It must have arrived unnoticed during the noisy main attack either just before I dived into the trench or while we were in residence. Either way, it was yet another lucky escape from death. The anti-personnel bomb consisted of a small bomb weighing about fifty pounds with a stick in the nose, which caused it to explode above ground level, shredding the air with shrapnel. They were dropped in canisters of four hundred at a time, and hence the sound of giant firecrackers when they all burst at the same time. A nasty weapon and very lethal. New aeroplanes were rapidly delivered, and we continued our operations.

A major battle for the town of Catania and the surrounding countryside, proceeded not far from us, and we could hear the artillery in front of us. Army casualties were heavy, and when we later went over the battlefield, there were many corpses and some sad scenes where a man's comrades had buried him with his riddled tin hat perched on his rifle as a marker. Bulldozers were burying the dead. Eventually the army broke through and continued on to Messina. This opened up a number of German fighter strips for inspection, and we soon were looking over some of the aircraft against which we had been pitted. We had to be very careful as mines, booby traps and all sorts of devices abounded.

We had a number of frights, one when I stepped on something which went 'crack', just like that made by the fuse of an 'S' mine. Everyone went flat. Another fright occurred when we tried to turn the engine of a ME 109 over with its starting handle. The guns all fired. We also found that the wings had had most of the main spar holding bolts removed, our 'friends' evidently hoping that when we flew it the wings would fall off. Ultimately we found an Italian Macchi 202 fighter in perfect condition, and this we later flew away for our enjoyment. When all had had a turn at flying it, the RAF presented it to the people of Malta. Unfortunately Jim Robinson crashed it on its delivery flight. I don't know whether it ever did reach Malta.

We had frequent clashes with enemy fighters over the Messina Straits when escorting our bombers, and on one occasion (28th August) we were attacked by ME 109s over the sea. In the ensuing mêlée, after shooting one down I found that I had latched on to a really experienced German pilot. He knew all the tricks, and after sparring around for a while trying to get onto each other's tail, we, by mutual consent, broke it off to look for easier prey. Perhaps I was getting lazy. Robbie happened to meet up with him, and a great combat occurred, concluding with the ME 109 crashing into a hillside while trying to out-manoeuvre Robbie in a ground level chase. That particular combat was reported on the BBC news. Robbie was a mass of nerves at the interview, and wanted to pull out, but we wouldn't let him.

On another raid, I ran out of ammunition while protecting our bombers (RAF Baltimores), and as the fight was still going on while the bombers were heading for home, I thought it would be a good idea to take a rest under the wing of one of them. This put me under the shelter and protection of their gunners. They were not amused, and made it plain by gesticulation (we were not on the same radio frequency) that my presence in that position was most unwelcome. Just then a ME 109 came diving down to the attack, and I went out to meet him despite being quite toothless, but he didn't know that. He dived away without firing, so the bomber crew could consider themselves lucky. I expect that it made a good story in the bomber mess that night.

While we were at Lentini, the ground forces moved on and forced the Germans into the Messina Straits area, and eventually across the Straits. Once again, with all the anti-aircraft defences bottled up in a small area, the AA flak became intense, and many aircraft including fighters were shot down. It was no pleasure to fly anywhere near the place, as even at 40,000 feet, intense heavy anti-aircraft fire was experienced, possibly at extreme range. But the shells still reached there and burst effectively.

A new base was being prepared for us at a place called Milazzo, right on the northern coast. It turned out to be a dusty, narrow, and fairly short strip, which was to house two squadrons of Spitfires. Once there we had our mess out in the open under some trees. It was very hot and dry at that time of the year, and this time we did not feel it necessary to excavate holes to shelter in, as we now had complete control of the air, and raids were not expected. We had taken over a large nearby building as sleeping quarters and we had several stretchers to each room. Vineyards surrounded us and I remember quite a few olive trees. Our moves were frequent, and this made it well nigh impossible for personal mail to catch up with us.

While I wrote regularly to my parents, I couldn't say much because of the censorship which required the removal of anything which described the war situation, or which might cause a drop in morale at home. So our letters were rather innocuous. It was rather galling to hear the BBC news service say that everything was quiet on the North African or Sicilian front, when there was one hell of a battle going on, both in the air and on the ground. Receipt of mail was a rarity, and I didn't receive mail from home for up to three months at a time, when a number of letters would arrive, all very much out of date. Parcels never reached us, except on one occasion when one arrived in Italy after chasing us on our trek through North Africa, Malta, Sicily, and finally Italy. It must have been sent when I was in England because it contained heavy white hand knitted stockings, a most welcome fruit cake which was dispatched in short order, and chocolate which had deteriorated to a powder and was not edible.

My recollections of Milazzo are that everything was very restful, with ripe grapes for the taking, and the Mediterranean Sea just off the end of the strip. The only thing to mar our life was that a war was progressing and we were not to forget it. A landing had been made across the Messina Straits, and no doubt to hurry things up, a landing to the north had been mounted at Salerno near Naples. Although we had had some warning, we were generally unaware that Italy was about to capitulate, and we were therefore surprised one day, while sitting at readiness, to see a Cant Z 1000 bomber appear over our strip with a white sheet fluttering out of a window. It made a most hairy landing on our strip, hitting a Walrus air-sea rescue amphibian on the way, but ending up relatively undamaged in a cloud of dust near some Spitfires at the end of the strip. The occupants were met as they disembarked and taken away, to where we did not know. No doubt they were well treated.

Cramming fighter squadrons on a small forward airstrip proved to be quite dangerous. One morning, having taken off on a sortie, I was just assembling my four aircraft above the strip, when on looking down, I saw two Spitfires of another squadron taking off down the strip in a cloud of dust while another Spitfire had started taking off in the opposite direction. There was not enough room for the aircraft to pass safely. I called out a warning over the RT but that wouldn't have done much good because it was too late to avoid an accident. It was quite horrible watching a terrible crash developing and being able to do nothing about it. The thought of three imminent deaths was wrenching. The three met and to my great wonder two of the Spitfires appeared out of the dust cloud flying out to each side of the strip while the single aeroplane rose, climbing straight ahead. To me it was a miracle. Presumably all the aircraft saw each other in time to use ground effect to get out of each other's way and remain flying under emergency power. None were so much as touched.

This reminds me of another remarkable incident back at Lentini. Off the end of one of our strips was a lake which was surrounded by high reeds. I was watching a Spitfire of another squadron take off one day, when at about 300 feet his aeroplane caught fire and the pilot baled out. His parachute, if he even tried, didn't have time to open, and he fell in a free fall trajectory down into the lake. A search party sent to find his body finally tracked him down unharmed except for being lost in the reeds. It seemed that the tall reeds had absorbed his fairly flat but high-speed fall, and he had skidded along the top of them before being deposited gently in the lake. Wonders never cease. So much for tall tales which are true.

It was during my time in Sicily that I became quite unwell. I was sitting at the mess table having just finished my evening meal when I suddenly felt very ill, and fainted while being helped to my billet. I awoke to see Whitamore standing over me asking if I had been taking my quinine pills. We took these daily to ward off malaria. I told him that I had. I was carted off to hospital at Catania where I was diagnosed as having clinical malaria. Sicily was a very bad place for malaria. The army doctors who had examined me later diagnosed yellow jaundice, now called hepatitis. I was transferred to a RAF hospital in Catania, and this turned out to be a terrible place run most incompetently in my opinion. After one day there, and still feeling ill, I and another officer were diagnosed as cured and transferred to a recuperation centre near the summit of Mount Etna.

We received no instructions regarding diet or anything else. Within a short time the other officer had a serious relapse and nearly died. I placed myself on bread and water under the supervision of a resident doctor for a month rather than return to such incompetent care in the hospital. I recovered and was duly released. My squadron had moved to Italy during my absence, and I had to set about finding it rather than report to a holding depot for a posting to another squadron. This proved to be no mean task.

14
Italy

While at the recuperation centre near the summit of Mount Etna in Sicily I had lost a lot of weight, and rather than hitch-hike to Italy by air to find my squadron, I thought that a trip by sea might prove interesting. Accordingly, I made my way to Palermo, a large town in northern Sicily, where I understood there was a naval base. Palermo was of course reputed to be the capital of the Sicilian mafia, but I saw no gangster-like characters with big hats as portrayed in the films. Upon arrival there in the morning, I asked for the Royal Navy headquarters, but the whole base seemed to be manned by Americans. I put in my request for transport by warship to Naples, and this was received quite courteously. I was told to come back in the afternoon and they might have something for me. Sure enough there was a Royal Navy launch leaving for Naples that evening, and I could go with her. A transport took me to the docks where I was shown a camouflaged launch of about 110 feet length. I was welcomed aboard, and we sailed at dusk in the teeth of a gale.

The launch was crewed by two officers and ten seamen, and was involved in anti-submarine duties.

When clear of land and at sea, a real storm developed, but I had no worries about seasickness as I had never before suffered from that debilitating condition. I ate a good meal in the wardroom and went to the bridge, but shortly after I didn't feel at all well and the dinner didn't last very long, I am afraid. The skipper and his second officer, with the usual naval courtesy, muttered something about losing their sea legs themselves, but the moment I left the bridge, probably laughed loudly at my expense. However, having lost my dinner, I felt quite well again and spent some time on the bridge chatting. Then the captain, a lieutenant, suggested that I might like to use his bunk as he would be on the bridge for the whole of the night. I gladly accepted his generous offer and slept soundly to wake up the next morning to a calm sea and a view of Naples from the entrance to the harbour.

The harbour itself showed many signs of damage, and I understood that it had just been taken over by the Allies. I enjoyed the generous and friendly hospitality of my naval friends and would like to make contact again, while realising that after the elapsed time span this is very unlikely. We docked at the main wharves, and I disembarked with very kind thoughts towards my hosts. I had nothing except what I stood in, so could not return their hospitality in any way. I then wandered the streets of the Naples waterfront, asking any servicemen I met if they had heard of or seen 81 Spitfire Squadron. The day passed without success, and I was beginning to wonder where I could spend the night. Naples was badly damaged and life had not returned to normal sufficiently to offer accommodation of any kind. I repaired to the wharves again, and met a naval officer who invited me to stay the night on his operations ship anchored in the harbour. Great was my relief, as Naples at that stage was no place to spend the night wandering about. Again I was given a great welcome, and had a very pleasant and safe night. The Royal Navy people were wonderful and gracious hosts and I really owed them a lot.

While on board the ship, my enquiries elicited the information that 81 Squadron was in Italy, but its precise whereabouts was unknown. Finally an RAF officer told me that he had heard that they were near Bari on the east coast. So I hitched a ride from the nearest aerodrome, and upon arriving at the other coast, I found out that 81 Squadron was based at Gioia near Bari. When I turned up I was received with great surprise but was still made most welcome. The usual procedure when someone took ill or left the squadron for whatever reason, was to report to a pilot's holding pool from which postings were made to squadrons which needed replacements. In contravention of this requirement I feigned ignorance and on this and a previous occasion had wended my way back to my old unit. No one seemed to object, and as very few broke the rules as I did, I seemed to get away with it. I was received back into the squadron and the adjutant had to tidy up the paper work. I kept away from liquor on the medico's instructions, but started to eat heartily to make up for my poor physical condition. Indeed I ate so much that I incurred the nickname of 'Porky', which stuck to me for the rest of my RAF career.

Life was quiet, and flying training was the norm, rather than operations. Things livened up a bit when the Italians laid mines on our airfield one night, and our CO, Babe Whitamore was blown up on take-off on a training flight with a new pilot on the squadron. His aeroplane was blown on to its back and it crashed inverted onto the grass surface, fortunately without catching fire. Whitamore crawled out of the cockpit through a very small hole, seemingly unhurt, and found time to castigate the new pilot for not continuing the exercise. Of course the poor blighter had landed back to find out how the CO had got on.

Orders then arrived for the squadron to ready itself for a move to the island of Kos in the Adriatic Sea and swift preparations ensued. We were ready to leave at dawn but the evening before, the Germans had dropped paratroops and captured the island, so our departure was hurriedly aborted. By sheer luck we had avoided landing 'in the bag'. This was followed by further orders to pack in a hurry for transfer to the Far Eastern theatre. We were told that we were to pick up new aeroplanes in Cairo, and were to fly them out to India. Apparently the RAF in India was in dire straits with the Japanese air force and, with 152 Squadron, we were to provide assistance. Our pilots and ground crew literally dropped everything and travelled to Taranto in the south of Italy, where we boarded a ship and sailed to Alexandria in Egypt.

Then we were taken by train to a holding camp in the desert just outside Cairo. This was definitely a temporary camp where we slept on stretchers in tents which were penetrated by sand with every breeze which blew. It was hot, dry and dusty. We were not there for very long but we still managed a visit to the town to see the sights. Cairo was as we had expected it to be. Masses of Arabs, and Egyptians intermingled with servicemen. Theft was common and one had to be alert. We didn't have an opportunity to visit the museum and other famous places as these were unfortunately closed. I and our other New Zealanders did however, manage to visit the Maadi base of the New Zealand Division where we acquired the peculiar New Zealand lemon squeezer hats. I wore mine throughout the later campaign even though we were subsequently issued with pith helmets with the RAF flash, and then with the famous broad brimmed Burma hats.

Our new Spitfires were to be picked up from Helwan aerodrome and flown to an assembly point on the Cairo West aerodrome. These were brand new Mk VIII aircraft, which were an actual advance on our old Spitfire Mk IXs. They were fitted with a new Rolls-Royce Merlin 66 engine with a Stromberg carburettor which allowed the aeroplane to fly inverted without the engine cutting out. They also had very clean lines with a retractable tail wheel, again an advance on the Mk IX. The engine of my aeroplane suddenly over heated and seized while on the way to Cairo West and I had to make a forced landing. I touched a sand hill just short of the runway and the resulting bounce just got me over the boundary fence onto the runway itself, so the aircraft was saved, not to mention my skin. I returned to Helwan for another Spitfire, which I delivered this time without mishap.

We were now shortly to leave the Middle East,

which I recall as a dry, dusty, and rather arid part of the world, where we had endured sustained and furious fighting with very little rest, at least for we fighter pilots.

15
India and Burma

We finally got away on our flight from Cairo to the Far East on 25th November, 1943. A flight of six Spitfire Mk VIIIs was escorted by a Blenheim bomber for navigation purposes, possibly they didn't trust us to be able to find our way. Our first stop was at Lydda airport in Palestine, where my aircraft was diagnosed as having a cracked engine block, so I was delayed. Then it was decided that my engine was in good condition after all, so I took off on the next leg with another six to a strip in the middle of the desert called H3 near an oil pipeline from Iraq. I heard that the Arabs used to drill holes in the pipe at remote locations to get free lighting fuel for their fires, and no doubt for other purposes, so that the pipeline, and other assets such as our aircraft for instance, had to be carefully guarded. This must have used up quite a number of our troops. Here we refuelled, and continued on to Habbaniyah, a permanent RAF station just south of Baghdad in Iraq.

We stayed the night there luxuriating in the facilities and protocol of an old world officers' mess, a pleasure we hadn't enjoyed since Britain, except that there it was a sergeants' mess. It was at

Habbaniyah that I found out the meaning of being blind drunk. We were very hot and tired after our flight and we were each given one small bottle of nicely cold Canadian beer to drink before dinner. That beer had a strange effect on me. When I sat down to dinner I was blind to the stage where I couldn't see what I was eating, but in other respects totally sober. It was a strange experience which I am glad to say hasn't been repeated since. I had great respect for the power of Canadian beer afterwards but never again had an opportunity to test its strength.

So far the topography was generally flat and the surface arid and sandy, even drier than North Africa. The next day we continued on to Shu'aiba in Kuwait where we refuelled again. A further hop that afternoon took us to Bahrain, the oil centre, where we spent another night. The coastline on the way to Bahrain was noted for changing its shape and position for up to thirty miles, so shallow was the sea there, and so subject to major wind and tide movement which is technically called slop. This was one of the reasons we had a navigating Blenheim. Our fuel reserves, even with a long-range tank fitted, did not allow much straying from the direct route. The topography was desert-like the whole way, and I didn't much fancy the idea of getting lost, or being forced down. Incidentally these long flights were far from comfortable for the Spitfire pilot who had to sit on a hard and lumpy survival dinghy the whole time. This dinghy was attached to the parachute equipment. After a long flight in a small and cramped cockpit without any opportunity for relaxation, one felt stiff and sore and tired.

From Bahrain we flew to Sharjah in Trucial Oman, still in desert landscape. As I recall it, Sharjah was just like one of the old desert forts described in the novel *Beau Geste*. It had solid stone walls and a large entrance gate which we were told was closed and locked at night. The sandy airstrip was just outside the walls; otherwise the fort stood on its own in the desert. I believe that Sharjah is a large and thriving town these days. Of course, the locals enjoyed regaling us with stories about the Bedouin tribesmen who roamed the desert outside, and who attacked the fort from time to time. I was most uncertain as to how much of this I could believe. Probably very little. Our aircraft were parked outside under guard for the night and we retired inside. The day temperatures were reaching considerable heights in the Arabian Gulf and we were really feeling the heat. On the ground so were the aircraft. An egg could be fried in seconds on the wing surface.

Our next leg was to a place called Jiwani across the Arabian Gulf, in Baluchistan. Our destination was an airstrip which seemed to be located in an old volcanic crater. Upon our arrival we had to circle round in a restricted circuit losing height until we could land on the strip. One could only describe the land as a moonscape; it was so dry and desolate. Large rocks were dotted around and there appeared to be no living things other than humans existing there. The heat was like a blast furnace. Once on the ground our engines had to be stopped almost immediately to avoid overheating, and our aircraft were pushed to their parking spots. We were told that this was a place of punishment for RAF men who had committed major misdemeanours, and I could well believe it.

The temperatures must have been in the 130s Fahrenheit with a very high humidity. We stayed there the night, and the next morning as I approached my aircraft I observed a fitter using a spanner through an access port to the engine. However, when he brought his hand out I could see no spanner. When asked where the spanner was, he denied having used one. Not further trouble, I thought to myself and asked for all the engine cowls to be removed for a search. The missing spanner was located in a position where it could fly around and do all sorts of damage. I did not know what happened to the guilty airman, as we had to leave. He deserved a severe punishment for his irresponsible action, which could have put my life in jeopardy, but I suppose that he was there for a similar or worse misdemeanour in the first place and was possibly past caring anyway.

We continued our journey and arrived at Karachi airport in the afternoon of the final day. That was our first major destination, and was to be our home for some considerable time while our machines were recamouflaged with jungle colours, and were thoroughly checked out. Incidentally, the jungle camouflage colours were chocolate brown and green, whereas those of the Middle East were different shades of gingery brown. No doubt the colours have special names, but we were never told. The undersides of the aircraft were always duck-egg blue to match the blue sky when looking upwards. The enemy had the same. The cowls just in front of the cockpit were always painted matt black to avoid reflected glare, and the leading edges of the wings plus the propeller tips were always painted a bright yellow.

Karachi couldn't be described as a favourite stopover. It was hot, dry, dusty and much smaller than we expected. Cows roamed the streets and bazaars without hindrance, and so did mangy looking dogs. We were accommodated in comfortable barracks however. Time dragged and the work on our aircraft seemed to merit no priority. There was a definite peacetime philosophy apparent. Breakfast was fairly late and leisurely, followed by morning tea, followed by tiffin (lunchtime), followed by a siesta of several hours, followed then by some hours of leisurely activity, and finally followed by drinks and tea before dinner. At least that was how we saw it. Our protests were answered with "You are in India now". We were told the war was suspended during the monsoon season, and even worse, that the financing of it by the Indian government was subject to a budget, and when the money ran out activity on the front was expected to stop. All quite unbelievable, but apparently substantially true. Prosecution of the war was the responsibility of the Indian government, which wasn't always in sympathy with the British Raj. All our sympathy went out to the poor soldiers, airmen and the navy, who had to do the fighting and put up with this. I doubt if the Japanese turned the war off to suit the conditions imposed by the Indian government.

Time went on and Mountbatten was appointed commander in chief, while the previous CIC, Wavell, became viceroy. Things changed for the better and the work on our aircraft was accelerated. While it seemed much longer, we took off on our final journey to the operational arena thirteen days after our arrival. The work should have been done in three days. Up to this point our whole journey had been over bare, arid and dune-like country, and we looked forward to something different. This proved not to be. The expected jungle about which one read as being the major feature of India, failed to materialise until well beyond Calcutta. Our first leg was to Jodhpur, about halfway to New Delhi, which was to be our stop for the night. The intervening country was regarded as hostile, with tribesmen dealing very harshly with any unfortunate infidel airmen who fell into their clutches. Various unmentionable indignities inflicted by tribal women on any unfortunate airmen who fell into their clutches were nevertheless mentioned and vividly described to us. We were issued with special passes called blood chits, which promised rewards to tribesmen for the safe return of British airmen in an undamaged condition. We took off for Jodhpur, again in a flight of six.

After take-off, a banging alerted me to an open hatch to the radio compartment, and I had to return to Karachi where the hatch was secured and my machine refuelled. I was aghast to find that it took far more fuel than expected, and I wouldn't have made it to Jodhpur if I had continued my flight. Visions of the blood chits lingered in my mind. The next day just before departure, I personally supervised the fuelling and made sure that all my tanks were full to overflowing. I took off with a new flight, and this time everything seemed in order.

My aeroplane flew for the full-calculated time on its long-range tank, but upon switching over to my main tanks, my fuel gauge started dropping rapidly. I was not unduly perturbed, knowing that all the tanks were full when I left, but I reported it to the flight commander nevertheless.

We were flying at 30,000 feet, and my gauge kept dropping until it showed empty. We had about thirty miles to go when my fuel light came on and my engine stopped. Below was the hostile desert mentioned earlier and I had no recourse but to continue in a glide for as far as possible. I trimmed for optimal gliding with my propeller in fully coarse pitch to reduce drag, and followed the others towards Jodhpur. I didn't think that I would make the whole distance even from 30,000 feet but as I neared Jodhpur it began to look as though I might be able to reach the aerodrome.

Jodhpur was the base for an elementary flying school using Tiger Moths which had no radio communication, so I asked the control tower to keep any other aircraft clear while I made my descent. I had to make a straight approach and landing and would be lucky if I could make it. I encountered a number of Tiger Moths making practice approaches right in my path. My speed of about 120 mph was much faster than theirs at 60 mph and I came up on one right in my path. The instructor saw me at the last moment and took evasive action, as did I by side slipping below. I had a clear view of both instructor and pupil and can only imagine their fright to find a fighter bearing down on them at high speed. The way opened up for me to land and I did so without mishap. A vehicle had to come out to tow me in to dispersal.

I stayed at Jodhpur for three days while engine fitters tried to establish the problem behind the fuel loss, without success. Every time the engine was started and run up, a tremendous amount of fuel disappeared. It couldn't be detected flowing out anywhere, nor could an excessive mixture be found to blame. Finally I decided to abandon the aircraft and continue my journey to Calcutta with the Indian National Airways in a De Havilland Dominie. It was quite pleasant sitting next to the pilot and chatting away while we slowly covered the ground. At Allahabad, where we stopped, I was beseeched to fly a Spitfire Mk V to Calcutta, but declined, which might seem strange. However, I had had so much trouble on the trip to India including two forced landings, that I felt that my flight just then was jinxed. I also had a distrust of the maintenance capabilities of Indian mechanics. Anyway, the Indian Airways pilot called out that he couldn't wait much longer for me to make up my mind, so I opted to continue with him. Today, I am surprised that I wasn't ordered to fly the Spitfire Mk V.

I finally arrived at the main civil airport of Calcutta, called Dum Dum, not too far behind my other more fortunate colleagues. After a short sojourn there, the whole squadron moved to Alipore airport on the other side of Calcutta. This, I believe was on about the 17th December, 1943. Our machines were placed under guard by Ghurkha soldiers, and we settled down to prepare for action. At this time we had no ammunition for our guns and fuelling was unreliable. So, it was rather annoying that Calcutta was raided by the Japanese while we had to sit on the ground and watch. The defending aircraft, some Hurricanes and Beau-fighters, were no match for the Japanese Zeros.

Christmas came and went. We were kept idle, which did allow us to enjoy some of the delights of Calcutta. The city is well known for its extremes of wealth and poverty, and this reputation is well deserved. It was most upsetting to see people begging for scraps of food, and the number of dead through starvation and other reasons, being carried off in carts for disposal each day. The streets at night were full of sleeping homeless people.

I had my first encounter with the life of wealth and opulence enjoyed by some members of the community, when I visited the swimming complex in Calcutta. I had just started undressing myself in a changing room, and had my shirt over my head, when I felt fingers fumbling with my belt. Expecting to find some thieving rogue about to rob me, I ripped my shirt off, to find a uniformed bearer protesting that the Sahib was undressing himself, and it wasn't done in this club. As an independent New Zealander, used to doing things for myself I didn't like the idea of being undressed by another person, and I explained to the bearer that I preferred to undress myself. He went off, no doubt wondering about the standards of these junior wartime officers. After having enjoyed the services of bearers, wonderful people that they were, I have often thought since, how nice it would be to have a personal servant at home.

At Christmas we had a wonderful party, at which everyone got blotto, or at least nearly everyone. Four of us were on early morning readiness so we had to go to bed early. The rest of our group came in during the early hours of the morning carrying one of our four, in an alcoholic comatose state. When we tried to get him up at dawn we couldn't rouse him. Walking him around the room just elicited his comment that his 'shank' wouldn't work. So, finally we put him back to bed and got some other poor blighter. Later, when we returned, we found out that he had a broken leg, and had been taken to hospital. Thereafter he was known as 'Shanks' McLean. He was a South African, of whom we had quite a number on the squadron. Some of British background, had no particular idiosyncrasies regarding coloured races, but those of Boer background did. However, they were careful not to display their abhorrence of coloured people in front of us. Most were very decent chaps.

Not much happened while we were in Calcutta, but the press was well aware of our arrival and gave us considerable publicity. One outcome was a request to demonstrate our fighters to a visiting Chinese delegation which was attending the racecourse that afternoon. We agreed with alacrity. It was arranged that a flypast would occur between races, and a low level high speed pass would be made by a single Spitfire. Larry Cronin was selected to do the high-speed pass. Timing was critical of course, and we were briefed as to the exact time our flypast should occur. This was also at low level. We did our part, but didn't allow for Indian foul-ups. Our flypast occurred just as a race started, and the horses bolted all over the course. Then Larry Cronin came down at 520 mph, and further chaos ensued. Very impressive, but hardly good for public relations. We were not asked to demonstrate again.

Shortly after that, we were sent east to the Imphal Valley in Assam. This was right on the border with Burma, and proved to be a most beautiful valley in the middle of a jungle covered mountainous range called the Chin Hills. The altitude of this valley was about 5,000 feet above sea level, while the mountains around towered up to about 8,000 feet or more. It was wintertime and the weather was excellent, as it is in most tropical countries in the winter season. It was very cold at night and frosts were frequent. Our clothing was tropical, our beds were bamboo charpoys, and we each had only three blankets. We froze. Much of the night was spent crouching over a fire to keep warm.

During the day we did patrols to familiarise ourselves with the area. There was no enemy activity. This pattern went on for several days, until one day nearly everyone went down with pneumonia-like symptoms. Most of us were taken to hospital where all but a few quickly recovered, but it put a whole fighter squadron out of action for approximately three days. Some of our people took a week to recover. Someone must have received a reprimand over the matter because we were immediately given adequate clothing and bedding.

The valley was dubbed Shangri-la and we enjoyed our stay there. Surrounding the valley were the hill tribes, the Nagas, Chins, Kachins, Karens and so on. The Nagas were thought to be headhunters and were paid a sum of money for each Japanese head brought in. I am not sure how each head was identified, perhaps by two ears, but in general they were supervised by an extraordinary young woman by the name of Ursula Graham-Bower, an anthropologist who had worked among the Nagas when war broke out. The Nagas were part of a British irregular force called V Force, and Ursula held the rank of lieutenant in this. She visited us one day with her body guard of armed Naga warriors and gave us an interesting talk on her activities.

The warriors were little men with tremendously muscular legs developed by their constant traversing of the steep mountain ridges comprising their territory. They looked quite primitive with their weapons but had a daunting reputation. I felt glad that they were on our side. It was comforting to be told that they had rescued quite a number of our airmen who had survived crashes in the jungle and who were hopelessly lost. We carried chits offering rewards to the natives for their handing us back to the British and we also carried a belt full of silver rupees as an aid to our assistance when on foot in Burma. In retrospect for the same purpose we also carried a belt full of gold francs when in Algeria.

The Manipur plains, which formed the bed of the valley, were peopled by a tall and statuesque race looking rather like Chinese. They were very friendly, although we did have some trouble with individuals. They crowded around each aircraft and appeared to be indulging in some form of worship. Each aircraft had its adherents, and these were so numerous as to impede our progress if we were scrambled into action. We didn't speak their language, and hand signalling with miming had no effect. Something had to be done. We solved the problem by shooting Very lights near them. As they ran we followed until they got the message and stayed away. Fortunately they had a sense of humour and it didn't adversely affect our friendly relations. They indulged in various festivals, some of which involved drenching anyone nearby with pink dye. I stopped such a sprinkling when I got too close one day watching the goings on. Whilst it didn't do anything to improve my rather skimpy uniform shirt and shorts, it was done with much laughter and good humour. And they were all drenched too! What it all meant was a mystery to me but it was all good fun.

Things were fairly quiet just then, and we could indulge in some recreation. The valley was some thirty miles long by ten miles broad, and contained a large lake (called Logtak), which teemed with wildfowl. I became friendly with a major in the local artillery, by name of Chaldecott, and we used to go on shooting expeditions. I had the only squadron shotgun (used by the pilots to practise snap shooting), a single barrelled weapon firing, strangely enough, New Zealand made CAC ammunition produced for skeet shooting. A protocol was observed wherein the local chieftain was given a spear, specially marked with our totem, and he sent it to the lake where it was planted in the ground to mark our campsite. Chaldecott and I would duly turn up to find our camp all ready for occupation, and canoes and paddlers waiting.

Payment for these services were made to the chief, except for the paddlers who were paid according to their performance and the success of the shoot. I cannot remember how much we paid. If one's shooting was not up to scratch, the paddler became quite surly as he saw his fee going down the drain. The shooting started with the evening flight, when the sky became black with wildfowl flying low overhead on their way to their night's lodging. If ready in time, one had only to elevate one's shotgun and fire vertically upwards to stand a good chance of hitting something. Ducks of several types, and geese were abundant.

On one occasion we missed the evening flight. Early in the morning the reverse occurred with the same black mass flying overhead on its way to feeding spots on the lake. We were late rising, and missed that too. However, later in the morning the Major and I, each in a separate canoe, set off to travel through the reeds in opposite directions around the lake, looking for duck. At the end of the day we would meet up again and compare bags, pay our paddlers, and return home. I found success hard to achieve because of some bad marksmanship, but really, I think, because of the unsuitable ammunition. It was interesting to see my canoe-er's attitude changing from pleasant to surly as he saw his reward diminishing with each miss. "Huzzoor!" he commented, "You not good today." There were other expressions but I couldn't speak the language. He was well paid anyway so didn't have much to complain about. However on one occasion, I collected more than thirty duck to the Major's six, and he, along with my canoe man was duly impressed.

The next night we had a terrific party with the nearby artillery battery as our guests. Of course duck was on the menu. A keg of Jamaican rum had been kindly donated by the Jamaican government (I have no idea how this happened but we didn't question such generosity) and the emptying of this down thirsty throats really gingered the party up. Later in the evening a game of indoor rugby, RAF versus the British Artillery, literally brought down our mess. The bamboo structure had to be rebuilt by 'tolerant' military authorities. Our artillery guests were poured or hoisted into their vehicles in the early hours of the morning, presumably to make their way safely home. We all had very sore heads the next day and for years afterwards I couldn't bear the sight of rum. I greatly enjoyed those shooting jaunts, and Major Chaldecott was excellent company. We were later to go to the Arakan to the south, and upon our return, things became quite hectic. I never saw Chaldecott again. I hope that he survived the war.

16
The Arakan

Following the débâcle of our hospitalisation with hypothermia, we received orders to fly down to the Arakan, which was about 1,200 miles to the south, and on the coast of Bengal. This was where all the current action seemed to be, as the Japanese army was pushing up the coast towards Calcutta. Much of the area in that region consisted of paddy fields, although further south the Japanese were being fought by our forces in thick jungle. We flew to a strip in the paddy fields called Reindeer 1, near Cox's Bazaar, and used that as our base while we were there. Facilities for flying, especially at night were zero. So was any provision for our welfare or comfort. I seem to remember that we shared the strip with another squadron, but I don't recall what they flew. Stories about the opposing Japanese fighters abounded, especially about their capabilities. We had fully considered these, and had decided on our tactics in combat, so were itching to try them out. Our Spitfire Mk VIIIs had high altitude, sharply pointed wing tips, something that we hadn't had past experience with. We were aware however, that at high speeds the aircraft became very hard to roll.

Immediately after our arrival we put up defensive patrols, but saw little. However, on 13th February, 1944, we intercepted a mass of Japanese fighters and had our first combat. The Japanese proved very aggressive, and were happy to defend against our attacks without heading for home. So, our combat time lasted much longer than usual. Upon our first attack they all flew in a giant circle, each fighter defending the one in front. We adopted our pre-determined tactic of diving to the attack and then pulling up to use our superior climb to gain height and position again. At the finish we claimed only a number damaged, but it became apparent later that many of these were reported by observers as crashed, so in fact we had scored quite a victory without loss to ourselves. Because our aeroplanes all had sharply pointed wing tips this allegedly gave us greater manoeuvrability at altitude. During one of my attacks I pulled up rather sharply to avoid a Japanese fighter which had latched briefly onto my tail, and I must have applied a lot of 'G' (centrifugal force). After I landed back at base, I discovered that my machine was quite badly damaged with extra dihedral, broken engine mounting, and tail rivets sprung.

A suggestion from my ground crew that I had made a heavy landing was not received with the jocularity it perhaps merited, because we found that many of the other Spitfires were similarly affected. We were all grounded while an investigation was carried out, and modifications made to the aeroplanes. One obvious change was the removal of our pointed wing tips and a reversion to the elliptical ones. I believe that the airframes were strengthened as well. We had no difficulties after that. Our sojourn in the Arakan lasted only ten days, but in that time the RAF gained air superiority over the Japanese air force, and the Japanese fighters started to run.

During this time I led an offensive patrol of six fighters on a reconnaissance over Akyab, a port held by the Japanese. On the way there flying low, one of the Spitfires hit the sea, and I thought that he was lost. However, he made it home safely despite a badly damaged propeller and engine. We had been briefed that there were no British naval craft in the area, so when we came across a naval launch on its own in broad daylight, we couldn't be blamed for concluding that it must be Japanese. However, I had a hunch that it could have been British. While I was strongly tempted to strafe it in passing, I told our people to hold their fire. We flew right alongside it and noted that it was flying the white ensign of the Royal Navy.

We left the launch untouched and reported it on our return, but to this day I am unsure whether it was a Royal Navy launch or a Japanese boat posing as one. If it was one of ours, the captain was probably unaware how close he came to being destroyed. I found it hard to accept the accuracy of intelligence briefings after that. The patrol was completed after encountering some miserable inaccurate anti-aircraft fire from the Japanese. We never did hear whether or not the launch was one of ours.

On one occasion I was part of a convoy patrol off the coast when four of us were kept on station, in spite of our protests, until after dark. We had no night flying facilities at our strip, nor did we have enough fuel left to fly to another base with such facilities. When finally released from our convoy duty night had fallen, and I led my colleagues in the general direction of where I believed our strip to be. It was pitch dark with no moon, and I didn't think we had a hope of finding it. That meant eventually baling out with the loss of four very valuable and scarce aircraft (Mk VIIIs were very scarce at that time). Ahead we saw Very lights being fired continuously, and I judged that someone was trying to help us. We had no radio communication with the ground, and we had to guess at what the person firing the Very lights intended. He was consistently firing them in a certain direction, and I assumed that this was the direction in which we were to land. Also the point where they were being fired from, I presumed was the desired point of touchdown.

Leaving my colleagues to circle, I made an instrument approach at a safe rate of descent aiming to hit the ground as close to the light source as possible. I hit the ground and of course the aeroplane immediately bounced. This was corrected and I kept straight on the landing run by instruments whilst braking as hard as I dared, and hoping that no obstacles were in the way. All of my guesses proved to be right, and with great relief, I looked around for someone to guide me back to the start of the strip runway.

A vehicle with a person holding a torch led me back to the start point and, after a quick chat with the person who had been firing the Very lights, I had him continue with this aid while I talked the others down by radio. All landed safely but one which crashed, but the pilot survived without much damage to himself. Altogether it was a stressful piece of flying, and excellent work by the chap who had exercised his initiative to provide us with the means of finding home and getting down. So far as I know, he received no recognition for his outstanding work. Nor, so far as I know, did the controller responsible for placing us in such jeopardy receive a deserved reprimand. For our part, it was accepted as just a normal incident of operational flying, but it did highlight what to us was an unacceptable attitude towards the value of fighters and their pilots, and displayed a lack of concern for our safety, let alone survival. We were not impressed, whatever the real reasons for holding us over the convoy for so long might have been. We were never told.

The Japanese offensive was being contained, and so was the Japanese air force. The RAF had a number of Hurricane and Spitfire Mk V squadrons which had been fighting the Japanese long before we arrived on the scene, and these chaps had had a hard time of it. But now with the advent of the Spitfire Mk VIII things were changing. More Spitfire Mk VIIIs were arriving, and more squadrons were being re-equipped, so the future was looking good. After a few more offensive patrols, and a few more combats, we were ordered to return to Imphal where a major offensive by the Japanese was expected. We duly flew back and settled down at Tulihal as our new base.

The runway was unsealed, and the monsoon was due to start. It soon became apparent that if we were to remain operational, we would need an all weather strip. Indeed we spent a day or two bogged down in mud at Tulihal. At the time I could not help but be astonished at the way the air war was being conducted without any apparent real understanding of the operational requirements of the modern fighter we had, and of the needs of the pilots flying it. That might seem rather critical but this was the second occasion on which we were prevented from operating effectively through inadequate support facilities.

Finally, someone must have realised how essential the few really capable fighter aeroplanes were in the theatre of war in the Far East. There were only two squadrons of Mk VIII Spitfires at that time. We were ordered to get off somehow and move to Kanglatombi, a new all weather strip comprised of netting laid on top of an earth runway. To get off Tulihal, with its mud, required a take-off within 600 feet of the start at the end of which was a small muddy lake of water across the runway. The available 600 feet was scraped clear of mud by a bulldozer and Whitamore, as the commanding officer, decided to go first. I followed. He opened his throttle wide with brakes on and two men holding his tail down. At a signal the two men pushed themselves clear into the mud, there wasn't much else they could do as the slipstream pinned them to the tail, and they had to push themselves off. The aircraft surged forward in a tail down position. Just before it hit the lake it lifted off and started to climb away. My turn next.

I did the same and kept my tail down, relying on engine power and ground effect to lift me into the air at the earliest possible moment. The aircraft wasn't actually flying, and it was necessary to translate the ground effect lift into aerodynamic lift as steadily and safely as possible. This meant keeping the aircraft close to the ground while the airspeed built up to the correct flying speed. This was accomplished and we had two aircraft away. I was permitted to advise my colleagues still on the ground of the technique I had adopted to take off, and we all got off safely. Kanglatombi turned out to be a pleasant home with new bashas, clean charpoys, and a flying strip with no unusual hazards. We settled down to our usual defensive and offensive patrols. The Japanese visited us occasionally, on which occasions there was usually a scrap. There wasn't a lot of risk for us as we were nearly always forewarned and able to position ourselves advantageously for an attack. We had a number of clashes during which I managed to add to my score on 16th March.

The well dressed fighter pilot wore accoutrements suitable for the particular conditions in which he operated. For instance in Britain the RAF's blue uniform or blue battle dress with revolver was the accepted garb. In North Africa we wore khaki battle dress with revolver and commando knife. But in India/Burma a little more was required because of the need to protect oneself if shot down into the jungle. The personal armament varied according to one's tastes. I wore the usual denim clothing with revolver but also had a commando knife, a dah (a long broad-bladed knife for cutting bamboo), and a sten gun with additional magazines. These were all fitted about my person without getting in the way. Fortunately it never became necessary to use them.

Now we come to Broadway. What follows is my version of a particularly nasty fight against superior odds, in which we lost Whitamore, Coulter, and Campbell, and lost all our Spitfires there but mine. For some years a squadron colleague kept reminding me to let him know what actually happened at Broadway concerning the Spitfire detachment there. He was finally given the version which comprised part of the early written memoirs of my war service. This account was included in a book subsequently written by him. Since that time I've been able to add more thoughts to what happened. While others might have observed from the ground the combat on 17th March, 1944, which had such drastic consequences, I was the only survivor of the aerial component, and the detailed memory of it is still clear in my mind. After all, when one has been subjected to forty minutes concentrated endeavour to kill one by a greatly superior number of foes, it tends to focus the mind and leave an indelible imprint. So here is my story of what happened on that fateful day.

17
Broadway

Broadway was the code name for an airstrip situated in an area of jungle and paddy fields near a bend in the Irrawaddy River in northern Burma, considerably north of Mandalay. Late in 1943 the Japanese were showing signs of advancing north to attack the British lines in the Chin Hills and the Imphal Valley near the border between India and Burma. Indeed by early 1944 they were pushing up the Tiddim road from the south and into the Kabaw Valley from the east. These were all areas heavily infested with jungle, noted for its denseness and its potential to inflict a range of nasty diseases on troops unfortunate enough to be based there.

The Kabaw Valley near Imphal had a particularly bad reputation for malaria, dengue, and much more, not to mention the many stinging, biting, sucking and invasive creatures usually resident in the jungle. Imphal was the main base for the British 14th Army in that area. It was a large valley nestling in the jungle clad mountain range up to 10,000 feet high, called the Chin Hills, and that was where we were finally based at an airstrip called Kanglatombi. Japanese air force activity was increasing and from Kanglatombi we, together with other fighter squadrons, ranged far and wide over the jungled Chin hills and western Burma.

Also at that time Brigadier Wingate, with a reputation for unorthodox tactics, was mounting his second Chindit expedition behind the Japanese lines in Burma. This predicated the use of several clearings with airstrips on which to land troops and supplies in the first phase of a major and sustained sortie into Japanese territory. Two of these strips were code-named Aberdeen and Broadway. At the last minute Aberdeen was found to be useless because of logs placed over the cleared area, but Broadway remained clear. Success of the whole exercise depended upon support from the air, supply to the troops on the ground and defence of the sky above.

From our point of view the Japanese air force was fairly active with bombers and fighters, and air defence at extreme range was going to have its difficulties. Timing was very important as operations during the monsoon season would be very difficult if not impossible because of incessant rain with mud and flooding making movement hazardous. Also, low cloud and poor visibility would aid the enemy in mounting aerial attacks on our Chindit bases. As it turned out Broadway became the central field base for the complete operation and it was defended against sustained ground and aerial attacks by the Japanese forces over the whole period while Chindit columns wreaked havoc in the surrounding Japanese held area.

At the beginning of the operation it was decided that Broadway should be defended by a detachment of fighters based there and initially Mustangs of the United States Air Force were given the task. This did not prove successful and Spitfires of 81 Squadron took it over. Thus the stage was set for our involvement in what turned out to be a very costly little exercise.

When given the task of defending Broadway there was some misgiving among the pilots about our ability to meet its requirements. The Broadway airstrip was approximately 200 miles behind the Japanese lines, too far from our Kanglatombi base to permit a return after a combat, and far from any other alternative airstrip. The Spitfire, while a superlative defensive fighter, had a short endurance and therefore a short range. This meant that there was nowhere else to go should Broadway come under sustained aerial attack and the defending Spitfires had to land to refuel and rearm. We would be quite exposed to the hazards of trying to land while under attack from enemy fighters and bombers. It was finally agreed that a detachment of six Spitfire Mk VIIIs, the very latest type outside Britain, would be based during the day at Broadway.

Our commanding officer, Squadron Leader Babe Whitamore DFC, would lead each detachment. The first six to go arrived at dawn and withstood several attacks by fighters and bombers with the loss of one Spitfire piloted by Sergeant Pilot Campbell, quite an experienced pilot very much liked by us all. He was shot down into dense jungle only a short distance from the airstrip but in spite of a search his crash site was never found. I was part of the six to go the next day, 17th March, 1944.

The weather was fine and we took off before dawn from our base at Kanglatombi. Our flight was led by Squadron Leader Whitamore with his number two, Pilot Officer Bill Coulter, myself with my number two, Flying Officer Bill Fell (RCAF), Captain Shanks McLean (SAAF) and his number two Lieutenant Tubby Gasson (SAAF). We flew almost due east on a course for Broadway over 200 miles of timbered Burma, a fairly arid stretch covered with teak forest. The flight there was uneventful and upon arrival at dawn we looked down on our base for the day, a short earth strip bounded on one side by jungle and teak forest, and on the other by dry paddy fields upon which lay the scattered remains of gliders and other debris of the first landing assault.

As I remember it the earth strip itself was only about 700 yards long, the minimum landing distance for a Spitfire, with obstacles at one end in the shape of a small pond and tall teak trees, and at the other end a swampy patch terminated by jungle. To land safely required what is called a precautionary let down at minimum flying speed aimed at touching down right at the start of the available landing run after a steep approach to avoid the tall trees. Then maximum safe braking was applied in the hope that one didn't end up in the swamp at the far end. With the Spitfire's long top-heavy nose, braking had to be very carefully applied. We all got down safely and parked our aeroplanes under cover of nearby trees.

Breakfast of a sort was supplied but mine was interrupted because I had unknowingly parked my aeroplane right on top of an unexploded bomb from a previous raid. Sure enough there was a hole directly under my Spitfire with the mangled fins of what looked like a bomb. I felt distinctly uncomfortable and exposed climbing into the cockpit, starting the engine, and taxiing to a safer spot hoping that the thing wouldn't go off while I was in the vicinity. The bomb disposal chaps arrived and wanted to know where it was. Reluctantly I showed them and was surprised and alarmed when they sat right on top of it to discuss how best to get rid of it. I was not impressed and, after nervously staying what I felt was a minimum period to avoid an accusation of cowardice, I used the very valid excuse that I had to have breakfast and left them to their dangerous task. They eventually blew it up!

I have the greatest admiration for those people with their cool nerve and bravery in dealing with such dangerous things. Our breakfast with its soy link sausages and tea made from a mixture of milk powder and tea leaves wasn't a culinary delight but it was certainly better than watching the disposal of a bomb from close range. In passing I shrink at the thought of those soy links which were our mainstay. They were like scented sawdust and just as dry.

It was unusual for such forward airstrips to have more than one or two light anti-aircraft guns such as Bofors for airfield defence, but Broadway had in addition a small experimental radar set which could provide some warning of incoming aircraft. It proved helpful but limited, as events would show. During breakfast a man came up to Babe Whitamore and said that the radar had picked up four aircraft coming in low and fast. About thirty miles away he said. Whitamore immediately ordered us to strap into our Spitfires ready for take-off. With this process completed we waited.

Our CO was faced with a difficult decision. If we all went off to meet the incoming four aircraft which could only be the enemy, we were open to being caught by a following raid while we were on the ground refuelling and rearming. If some of us were left on the ground to later provide cover for the aircraft refuelling, they could be subject to attack from the oncoming raiding force. Meanwhile reports were still coming in describing the four attackers as getting closer. Whitamore eventually decided that only he and his number two, Coulter, would go off leaving the remainder of us to wait at readiness on the ground. Both started their engines and then Whitamore, changing his mind, signalled to me to start up and go with him instead of Coulter, thus as it happened saving my life.

Babe led me out onto the strip and immediately started his take-off with me following closely behind. He had left the ground and was raising his undercarriage while I was still on the strip just reaching flying speed when four Japanese Oscar fighters flew right over the top of us making straight for the other Spitfires. They passed over me by only a few feet it seemed. Whitamore did a very risky stall turn virtually off the ground to try to follow the Oscars while I pushed my throttle right through the gate for absolute maximum engine power and tried to follow. Neither of us managed to get sufficiently around to get at the Oscars so we clambered for height. Both of us managed to reach something like 2,000 feet and rolled out from an inverted position to find enemy fighters all around us.

There must have been at least twenty of them
unreported by the radar. They were the top cover
for the four initial attackers and caught us
completely by surprise. Whitamore was transmit-
ting on the radio, presumably instructing the
Spitfires on the ground, so I was unable to speak to
him. He was obviously aware that we had far more
company than the originals and he was firing at an
Oscar right in front of him unaware that three more
were right on his tail firing at him. Action sequences
were happening so rapidly that in terms of time we
are talking here about fractions of a second to
assess a situation and to act.

I turned to go to Whitamore's assistance and in
doing so became aware that I also had three or
more lining up on my tail. Indeed one of these was
so close that I could see the yellow strips along the
leading edges of his wings and smoke dribbling
back from his guns as he fired at me. Before I could
get even close to Babe Whitamore the aeroplane he
was firing at burst into flames but he also abruptly
ceased talking on the radio. That was the last I saw
or heard of him as I had to do something immediately about my pursuers. He must have been
killed outright by one of the three shooting at him.
I now had something like two dozen enemy fighters
all to myself and bent on my destruction.

They seemed to be everywhere, above, beside,
and more importantly behind. I felt acutely aware
that I had nowhere to go and hoped that the
superior performance of my machine would see me
safely through. However it transpired that it didn't
help to outdistance the opposition because they had
altitude, numbers and position, and at no time did

they relinquish that state of affairs. It became the classic dogfight at low altitude with an opposition more manoeuvrable and nearly as fast. My advantage was speed (but not acceleration) and power, plus possibly armament, if I had the opportunity to use it. The whole charade took place at little more than 0-2,000 feet as all the enemy fighters had me hemmed in. Only one opportunity to hit back occurred when one of the Oscars tried a head-on attack and we both fired at each other. I saw cannon strikes on his fuselage before he shot past and the army later confirmed to me that he had crashed.

To prevent the fighters on my tail from getting a telling burst into me became my top priority, and I hauled my aeroplane into a steep spiralling climb whilst skidding and slipping to make myself a hard target to follow. At the top I flipped over into a steep dive at maximum power while aileron turning with slip and skid. At the last moment I pulled the aeroplane out at maximum gravity force and with satisfaction saw that I had lost the crop on my tail. We had heard that because of the peculiarities of centres of gravity and centres of pressures in Japanese aircraft their pilots had greater difficulty in absorbing the deleterious effects of G. I used this hopefully to get rid of my followers. They were so manoeuvrable however that I doubted if any had hit the jungle. Each time I attempted to out-speed them others came from altitude to latch onto my tail again. The same occurred when I tried to out-climb them.

So the whole combat became a mêlée of mad flying on my part with no chance of hitting back. As

I had nowhere I could go to it all took place within a few miles of the airstrip. The only positive aspect was that while they were engaged trying to shoot me down they could not be attacking the ground installations or our people on the ground. As in a boxing ring with no round breaks, fatigue began to set in. The business of such combat as dogfighting takes considerable physical effort with the use of arms, legs, eyes, and head, and it wasn't long before I began to feel really tired. I worried lest through fatigue I finally became a victim to the enemy efforts. I preferred a possible escape from a crash landing in a clearing rather than through sheer fatigue have some Japanese achieve the thrill of shooting me down, so I began to watch for a suitable gap in the jungle. This I discovered in one of my low passes although it didn't seem to offer much hope of a safe haven. Before seriously contemplating such an escape, I decided to attempt one last desperate shot at my opponents but couldn't see any. They had simply called the whole thing off and disappeared, probably because of fuel shortage. The Oscars had a much greater endurance time than the Spitfire but they also had quite a distance to fly back to their base.

I returned to the airstrip to find fire seemingly everywhere. Obviously some of the fighters had been strafing. I landed without mishap and got out of the cockpit in a very tense condition which I relieved by running around until my nerves quietened down. While in this mode I remember going along a jungle track when I came across a senior army officer under a tree waving his revolver around enquiring, "Where are the bastards?" The thought of a revolver shooting at a modern fighter seemed so ridiculous, and I remember saying something along the lines of, "Don't be such a bloody fool" which he very kindly ignored. It might have been Brigadier Calvert!

Upon enquiry, I was shocked to find that Pilot Officer Bill Coulter whose place I had taken at Whitamore's request, had been badly wounded in the first attack by the four Oscars and all the Spitfires left on the ground had been destroyed, fortunately without the loss of their pilots. Bill died of his wounds shortly after receiving them. My flying time was booked at forty minutes, so no wonder I felt exhausted. My aeroplane, when I looked at it, wasn't all it should have been. The tail rivets were sprung, the wings had extra dihedral, and the engine mounting was damaged. A hole behind the cockpit showed where a cannon shell had entered. One of my opponents had been lucky. The shell had exploded under the seat and armour plate had given me protection. It was still flyable however, and I flew it back to Kanglatombi to be greeted by my squadron colleagues who had not yet heard the sad news – the loss of our commanding officer and another of our pilots with all of the aeroplanes except mine destroyed.

Shortly after my arrival I informed by telephone our air officer commanding, Air Vice-Marshal Vincent of this most recent episode at Broadway and he ordered the immediate abandonment of the detachment there. Thereafter the air defence of Broadway was carried out by scrambling Spitfires when an attack was reported or was known to be imminent, but because of the distances involved this was not really effective. Fortunately it didn't seem to affect greatly the supply situation for the Chindits as the C47 Dakota supply aircraft were always escorted during daylight hours.

The loss of Squadron Leader Whitamore was keenly felt by the squadron and even more by the upper hierarchy as they had him marked for higher things so we were told. He was a brave and able fighter pilot whose great misfortune, like Coulter, was to be in the wrong place at the wrong time. His crash site, like that of Sergeant Pilot Campbell, was never found, even though a thorough search was mounted. The jungle was just too thick. Coulter was the least experienced of us and I suppose should never have been there in the first place.

For me the episode was one which tested all of my skills, experience, and knowledge as a fighter pilot. I was most fortunate on several counts. My respect for the wonderful and dependable Spitfire was increased greatly. We had to do things with those aeroplanes which must have exceeded the aerodynamic and physical limits quite often and they never let us down. Much later I did take unjustified liberties with my aeroplane and it reacted severely with nearly fatal results, but that is another story. In view of the results, the detachment to Broadway could hardly be called a success. It did emphasise to all that modern fighters could not operate effectively without adequate warning devices or when isolated from alternative landing strips. We were given a new commanding officer Squadron Leader Marshall, a very nice and able man who was later killed in an aircraft accident after I left 81 Squadron.

18

The Japanese Invasion
of Imphal

We were at readiness one day at Kanglatombi after
the Broadway incident, when shells started bursting
on the Imphal airstrip just across the valley from us.
This was the first sign that the Japanese had reached
the Imphal Valley. We ourselves were not under
direct fire, and from such a safe position it was
amusing to watch the panic reaction, with people
running everywhere, and aircraft hurriedly taking
off. It appeared that the Japanese had brought
artillery for many miles through the jungle past our
defending troops to get in behind our base forces at
the Imphal aerodrome, from where they rained
shells down on the unsuspecting RAF and Army
headquarters. I cannot remember how this attack at
our very heart was dealt with but no doubt our
troops eventually rooted the Japanese out of their
position.

Then started a period of activity where our strip
was exposed to attack by enemy troops, and this
required us to standby over night with rifles and
sten guns. One air strip at Palel further down the
valley, housing Hurricane squadrons, was attacked

and much damage was done. Because of our vulnerability to heavy damage by enemy ground attack it was decided to move us in a hurry to the next-door valley to the west, over the jungle covered hills. This was called the Silchar Valley, and our new all weather strip was called Khumbhirgram. The strip was surrounded by heavy jungle on all sides, but the valley itself had quite a few tea plantations. Real civilisation at last!

Silchar town was the social centre, which had a club where the local British residents gathered for recreation. Around the walls were paintings of past presidents who were nearly all high-ranking army officers. We wryly noted that they all had the letters VD after their name. Of course it meant 'Volunteer Decoration', but in wartime it had a much different connotation and with our juvenile sense of humour we enjoyed the inference. We met the local tea planters and enjoyed their generous hospitality which introduced me in particular to the wonders of whisky. I have appreciated it ever since.

Spirits were the vogue for a good reason. The water was so bad and dangerous to drink that a good injection of spirits killed off most if not all the dangerous bugs. Of course it also made drinking water enjoyable, and with the high temperatures and humidity we had to drink a lot of liquid. Indeed most of our life in India and Burma was spent in a saturated condition, especially during the monsoon season. This was hard on our clothing which came apart after a relatively short time when the threads rotted. At Khumbhirgram Indian tailors were available and rotted clothing could be replaced quite easily. Anyway we usually only wore shirts and shorts when not flying, and long sleeved shirts and trousers when flying.

The Khumbhirgram strip was inhabited by a Vengeance dive-bombing squadron, strangely enough number 82 Squadron, RAF. Our accommodation was in bashas, which were bamboo huts, but we had a concrete structure as our mess, and could enjoy the pleasure of sitting at a table for our meals. We had bearers allotted to us and for the first time we began to enjoy a reasonably pampered life as officers of a rear echelon unit. I had to pay my personal bearer a monthly salary of forty rupees, and in return he kept the basha which I shared with Larry Cronin, clean and tidy, and prepared an evening bath for me. He even kept the mosquitoes (which swarmed prolifically) off me while I washed and bathed.

Our sleeping quarters were quite some way through the jungle from our mess, and frequently while making our way there after an evening's relaxation, we would be confronted by a panther. We were not permitted to shoot wildlife in case wounding created a problem of man-eating carnivores, and I discovered that shining a torch in the eyes of the panther would ultimately cause it to retreat into the surrounding jungle. There was also a large cat called a chindval, which looked like a small lynx which we frequently encountered on our jungle path.

While we were there, no problems with the abundant wildlife surfaced.

Violent monsoon storms occurred frequently, and our bashas suffered badly. The one I shared with Larry Cronin one night must have been in the path of some very small but vicious migrating ants. I came to bed late and my charpoy was in the path of millions of the little brutes. Larry had a charmed life and his bed was in the clear. While getting undressed in the dark they ran all over me in their thousands and stung savagely. Once I had managed to get into bed they swarmed over my mosquito net, dropping through and biting me. I had no sleep with trying to ensure that they stayed out of my mouth and nose all night.

The next day I poured petrol through our basha to get rid of the things, and placed the feet of my charpoy in tins of kerosene to protect me in future. Larry, strangely enough was not affected by any of this and to my chagrin was not very sympathetic either as I had disturbed his sleep with my very justified complaints. The place had all sorts of denizens from scorpions to mosquito eating lizards which had a loud and an interesting call.

It wasn't long before our basha was destroyed by a monsoon storm, and we ended up in a tent. At that time the squadron had two little dogs called Naga terriers, as pets. One night I was asleep in my tent with three others. My revolver was hanging at the head of the bed. I was awakened by the tent shaking, and I heard snarls outside. Then a sniff at the tent wall next to my ear occurred. I actually considered bashing the tent wall where the sniffing happened but was deterred by the thought of a big paw full of claws having a go at me. There seemed to be two panthers patrolling the area around the tent, and one must have disturbed a guy rope. It actually entered the tent, but went out again. I couldn't access my revolver, and perhaps it is as well that I didn't. The two panthers went away, and later at dawn, I discovered that one of the Naga terriers was sleeping under my stretcher. Dogs are apparently a delicacy for panthers, and this was what had attracted them that night. It was only the presence of humans which deterred them from taking our Naga terriers.

All in all at Khumbhirgram we enjoyed quite a social life when free from the demands of war. We were the guests of the tea planters at various times. They were wonderful hosts, if rather hardened whisky drinkers. We once played a rugby match against some commandos who were carrying out exercises in the vicinity. The contest was played at Silchar in monsoon conditions of high temperatures and high humidity, and we lost. I played as hooker, and the two things that I remember most were the handfuls of wet mud which my opposing hooker persisted in slapping into my face whenever I had a chance to win the ball, and the commanding officer of the commandos, a colonel, running up and down the sideline calling out to his 'boys' as he called them, to massacre us. Ah well! I suppose when you play very mobile gorillas, you can expect to have a hard time. And there was always the hospitality of the Silchar Club available as a final panacea.

The base at Khumbhirgram was too far from the scene of action to be fully effective, but nevertheless we still managed to keep the Japanese air force opposed, together with valuable assistance of other RAF squadrons, of course. One of our main tasks was to protect supply aircraft feeding Imphal, which was under siege. We had to keep an aerial corridor open, along which C47s flew. So did other aircraft, and one day I was on patrol with my number two when we were vectored by the controller onto a bogey aircraft (an aircraft of unknown identity), which turned out to be an American B25 bomber. It fired at us as we came up close to investigate it, and I told my number two "Keep clear. The bastards are shooting at us", or something along those lines. This was picked up by listening radio units and duly recorded. My language must have caused some comment because it has since been quoted in a book or two about the RAF in the Far East. What interested me was the said bomber reported being attacked by two Japanese fighters who it then shot down. So much for the accuracy of some American claims.

On April 17th we were scrambled from the strip myself leading B Flight of four Spitfires. We soon intercepted six bombers at 15,000 feet, with covering fighters up to 30,000 feet. We positioned ourselves and then attacked the top cover. At high altitude the Japanese aircraft performed poorly in comparison with the Spitfire and they rapidly joined their medium cover fighters. This is where the main combat took place.

The Oscar I claimed destroyed was badly hit and fell out of the sky obviously out of control. It spun, recovered, spun and recovered in that sequence until a gout of flame appeared from the jungle well below. I was assembling my flight for a further attack when one Oscar came from underneath, firing at me until he could climb no more and stall-turned away. As we were reassembling I only took evasive action and did not press this further good opportunity.

At Khumbhirgram some of the operational pressure had decreased and there was time for leisure activities. It occurred to me that I could have some fun at the expense of my colleagues. I arranged with my ground crew to remove the propellant from a 20 mm cannon shell, substitute sand, and then replace the armour piercing head, so that no-one would know that the cannon shell wasn't live. I then borrowed a hammer and awaited my opportunity. When a group of our pilots were together chatting at dispersal I appeared with the shell and hammer and started to whack the sensitive head of the shell with the hammer while at the same time expressing great surprise that nothing was happening. This was the quite understandable behaviour of a pilot suffering a mental breakdown.

As I approached the group they all took to their heels telling me to stop being so stupid. I kept up the charade, and eventually one of my colleagues came over to me making placatory noises, and asked to have a go at it himself. I demurred but under his persuasion handed the shell and hammer over to him, whereupon he hurled the shell as far as he could into the jungle. I collapsed with laughter and explained to the others how they had been had. I must admit that most of them didn't see the funny side at all. To me the chap who had relieved me of the explosive shell had shown great courage in coming up to me in what to him was a very dangerous situation, and had acted to save a tragedy. I nevertheless had enjoyed the spoof, but had taken a risk of being declared as suffering a mental breakdown. I had to show them how the shell had been deactivated before they were prepared to accept that I was still sane. All in all, a bit of enjoyable fun, for a few of us anyway.

It was at Khumbhirgram that I had my last serious joust with the grim reaper. Previously, I have mentioned that it was a rare occasion for ground crews to let one down. This was partly the reason for the following incident. As I said before, the Khumbhirgram strip was surrounded by dense jungle for many miles, and there was nowhere else to put down in the event of an emergency. The squadron on this occasion was taking off on an operation requiring the use of long-range tanks. It was customary to complete cockpit take-off drills before leaving an aircraft after the last operation, so that the aeroplane was ready for an immediate scramble if required. Therefore it was expected that the aircraft were ready for take-off on this particular sortie. The ground crew were responsible for seeing that aircraft were fitted out and ready for the next operation. So on this occasion I jumped into my aircraft without an all round inspection, and took off with the rest of the squadron. I immediately switched over to my long-range tank and the engine cut. There was no hope of it starting again because of the peculiarities of the Stromberg carburettor, and at about 200 feet I was faced with a most serious situation.

It was not possible to glide around the circuit to make a normal forced landing. It was suicide to try to make a 180 degree turn back to the strip to land. Many dead pilots can testify to that mistake. A crash into dense jungle seemed a certainty. I recall my conclusion that I had a zero chance of survival, and the sense of panic that this generated. I had to fight against trying to do something silly. Training took over, and I converted my excess speed into extra height while trimming my aircraft to its optimum gliding condition. I had had practice at this before. I put my propeller into fully coarse pitch to minimise drag, and then carried out a gentle turn parallel to the runway. My number two came alongside enquiring what was wrong, and as I was too busy to tell him, I just sent him off out of my way with a curt order. I hoped to get as far around the circuit as possible before having to carry out a desperate manoeuvre as a last resort.

To my great surprise I found that by the time I had everything sorted out, I was in a position to make a normal forced landing back onto the strip. My approach was complicated by a tractor choosing to tow a Vengeance dive-bomber across the end of the landing strip thus blocking it to me. So it became necessary to land on rough ground adjacent to the sealed runway. This wouldn't matter as I intended to do a wheels up landing anyway. At the last minute I found that I had too much altitude, and I had to do some violent fishtailing to lose the extra height. As I levelled out to land I decided I had time to lower my undercarriage and I activated an emergency lowering device which used compressed air to force the undercarriage down quickly. Nothing happened, and I quickly glanced at the lever I had operated, only to find that it had not travelled through its whole distance. A further bang on the lever, a hiss, and the aircraft touched the ground with the undercarriage down.

I was extremely lucky to survive in the first place, and to save the aircraft without damage in the second place. My plane rolled to a stop, and a fire tender with our engineering officer turned up. I climbed out rather shaken at my escape, and to this day I have no idea how I managed to get my aeroplane to glide around a whole circuit with height to spare from such a low start altitude. Something must have supported me. The alternative was certain death. Strangely, no one said anything and treated the episode as quite normal, even though numerous pilots in the same sort of position had been killed. My ground crew were very upset because it transpired that they had removed my long-range tank without telling me, and of course when I had switched my fuel supply to it, the engine had tried to run on air. I still regard this episode as one where my flying knowledge, air discipline, and self-control were most severely tested. (I have since concluded that powerful thermals might have had a hand in keeping my aircraft aloft around the circuit.)

Shortly after this, I was sent on a course to the Central Gunnery School, RAF, at Armada Road west of Calcutta. This course taught all that was known about the best techniques available for aerial combat and gunnery, and was quite demanding in the sense that a number of trainees crashed while carrying out some of the difficult exercises. I passed out with an 'A' pass rating, and returned to the squadron itching to try out my newly learnt skills. This was not to be. I had no further combats with enemy fighters, although we did quite a bit of strafing in the jungle around the Tiddim Road, and bordering the Chindwin River.

The enemy used to hide camouflaged supply dumps in the jungle and it was our job to find them and destroy them. It was when flying down the Tiddim Road that I was hit in the wing by an unexpected burst of enemy AA fire. While quite a number of strafing aircraft received hits, I was generally rather lucky. It was quite a business flying low along steep ravines with mountain ridges on either side or circling down into tight valleys to find and strafe the enemy supply dumps. Only a powerful aircraft like ours could do it safely against opposition.

One last comment about the weather conditions during the monsoon period. These were recognised as being some of the worst in the world. Flying in and out of the Imphal Valley over mountainous ranges during this period was downright dangerous. One could depart in reasonable weather to find on one's return, storm clouds down over the mountain ridges and heavy rain and turbulence sufficient to destroy an aircraft. One had then to find one's way through narrow valleys back into the Imphal Valley. There was no alternative. Many aircraft were lost and pilots killed under these conditions.

One other aspect of the air war in the Far East should be recorded. Since the great retreat from Singapore, RAF fighter pilots had to fight against the Japanese with antiquated aircraft which were outclassed by their opponents. They did this for years without proper recognition or assistance. It is a tribute to their tenacity, bravery, and ability, that they survived the onslaught in the face of terrible conditions and neglect, without an apparent serious fall in morale. We arrived on the scene very late, and with machines which at last could outclass the enemy.

Two more incidents remain in my memory. The first concerns a trip down the Tiddim Road looking for business, when I came across a small truck full of Japanese soldiers just where the road curved into the mountainside. The soldiers all baled out, but one did a spectacular dive and landed on his head. He just lay there the whole time I spent trying to strafe the truck. Unfortunately this proved impossible because of the inaccessible position of that part of the road which ran half way up a steep ravine with the opposite steep mountain wall only a short distance away. Try as I might, I couldn't get a shot at the target without crashing. While I was flying up and down the gorge an AA gun opened up from the Tiddim village and hit me in the port wing. Fortunately the aeroplane was still flyable and in a rage I sprayed the suspected location of the gun with cannon and machine gun fire. It didn't open up again, but I doubt that I hit anything.

The second incident concerned elephants. Tame elephants were used extensively by the British for a wide variety of purposes in peacetime and early in the Eastern war. They were also used by the Japanese later on, and were considered indispensable in the conditions of mud and difficult terrain. We were specifically forbidden from killing these elephants because they would be very useful to the British when they returned to Burma. We were however, permitted to stampede herds of wild elephants which were occasionally found corralled by the Japanese deep in the jungle. It was interesting to frighten these creatures by flying low over them. The only occasion I did this caused them to break out of their confinement, and to stampede through the jungle like a tidal wave. After splitting them up we left them alone. However the time came when we received orders to kill the tame elephants to keep them from the Japanese.

My number two and I found two tame elephants bathing in the Chindwin River with their mahouts on their backs. One was actually in the river and the other was on the river bank. I took the one in the river and my number two the one on the bank. The mahouts, realizing their danger, slipped off the backs of their elephants and got clear. My cannon shells hit the elephant squarely and it must have been killed instantly. At the same time two Hurricane fighters came from nowhere and tried to shoot the other one. There were some pretty harsh words before the second elephant was dispatched. I felt very bad about this, because I felt that it was really the murder of an innocent animal, and I never wished to participate again. Fortunately the Japanese advance was stopped at Kohima and their retreat was begun with costly losses. The shooting of elephants became unnecessary from then on.

19

Retirement

Quite without warning we were sent to Ceylon. The explanation was that we were to be re-equipped with American Thunderbolt fighters which had a much greater range. This seemed logical because the nature of the war in the Far East had changed, and the Allies were now on the offensive. With vast distances involved, the Spitfire, which was a superlative defensive fighter, but had a short range and endurance, would be unsuitable. We packed up in the manner to which we were so accustomed, i.e. very little personal gear with us in our aeroplanes, and took off in two flights on the long journey to a strip called Minnerya in Ceylon. This meant flying down the southern coast of India with an overnight stop at a place called Vizagapatnam.

At the time I was suffering from a bad attack of jungle ulcers on both legs. These were very painful open sores which started as an itching pustule, but which became open and painful. I do not know what caused them, but they were a common affliction in the Far East, and very hard to cure. Perhaps it was long hours in the cockpit while sweating profusely. Mine occurred up the backs of my legs up to and including my rump. The medical people tried all sorts of coloured paints such as acriflavine, mercurichrome, and gentian violet, without success, until a coal tar dye called brilliant green (which it was) finally worked. A large part of me was like a rainbow. With the others, I had to fly in this condition, and I found it rather uncomfortable. I had also contracted a virulent type of impetigo on my face. This could be watched spreading and the treatment consisted of ripping off the infected skin with tweezers and the application of some stinging sort of lotion. The whole of one side of my face plus my moustache area was infected within hours, so that the above treatment hardly left me with an attractive visage.

The long flight went off without trouble, but another squadron on the same journey ran into a cumulonimbus cloud on the way and most of them, including their CO, did not survive. We were shocked. The details of this tragedy have been recorded in several books. I have mentioned before the savagery of the monsoon flying conditions, and this was just another example. It seems that I was fated to have an incident on each long flight, and this was no exception.

On the leg from Vizagapatnam to Minnerya, with a refuelling stop in between, we were delayed and had to complete the last stage at night over heavy jungle covering much of northern Ceylon. While flying over this jungle in the dark, my engine suddenly stopped and burst into flames. At the same time all my electrics failed, so that I had no radio nor lights of any kind. The flames were coming back right over my cockpit canopy, and it was time to get out. I released my harness, and was preparing to evacuate at about 10,000 feet when the fire went out, and my engine showed signs of restarting. After some checking of fuel cocks and instruments it seemed that I might have some power again, so I settled down to fly on. My problem now was rather different.

My destination was a strip in the jungle about which I had little information, and which I had never seen. I still had no electrics so had no communication. The others of course, had flown on and were some distance ahead. I had to find the strip in the dark, had somehow to alert the control authorities that I wasn't an unfriendly alien, and had to persuade them that I wished to land. Without any other option, I continued my original course, and finally was rewarded with the appearance of lights in the distance, which turned out to be an airstrip with a landing flare path turned on. This could only be Minnerya.

Having no navigation lights or any other means of making my presence known, I had to stay clear of the landing circuit until I was certain that all of my better equipped comrades were safely down, and then I flew low down the strip, hoping that they would see my Spitfire in the flare path lights, and leave them on for my landing. The ploy worked and I made my landing safely. Our engineering officer never did give me an adequate explanation for the fire and failure of my electrical systems, but I suspect that he was too busy to spend much time on the problem anyway. I had only one more flight with my squadron, and that in a machine different from the one I had flown from India.

Pilots from the squadron were posted to other

positions immediately after our arrival, and they, including my special friend and comrade, Larry Cronin, just seemed to disappear. There were no functions or parties, and it was a terrific anticlimax for me, and no doubt others. After years of operational service with 81 Squadron, we were 'given the boot' so to speak. I spent a week there doing nothing but enjoying a restful time walking the jungle tracks and watching the wildlife. Monkeys abounded and small faces would peer out at me as I passed by on the narrow tracks. On a nearby riverbank there were giant lizards which seemed to be about six feet long sunning themselves. These moved with great rapidity into large holes when they saw me. I wondered what they were, but had no way of finding out.

During this time I received my posting, which was to Poona in India, a town made famous in novels and history books for its depiction of the English lifestyle under the British Raj. My first thought was that I had no proper uniform, and no means of getting one. Our clothing had been a minimum required for flying and living in hot, steamy and sweaty conditions in Assam, and usually fell apart when the sewing threads rotted. I had been promoted to flight lieutenant, and was to take command of a flight which trained all incoming fighter pilots in combat tactics and aerial gunnery. Apparently a colleague who had attended the Armada Road course with me had requested my presence at Poona. I left the squadron which had been my home since November 1942, with a sad heart.

I travelled by train to the north of Ceylon, and

thence by ferry to Madras, where I caught the
Madras to Bombay express. It was an all day
journey as I remember it. I had lunch in the dining
car and ordered a ham salad believing the food on
such a well-known and illustrious express would be
safe. Not so. The ham was bad and I had only a
mouthful before spitting it out. However it was too
late and I caught dysentery which continually
hospitalised me after I reached Poona. I was at
Poona for three months, most of which seemed to
be spent in hospital with continually recurring
attacks of dysentery. My weight went down to
about eight stone, and I began to wonder if I would
make it home. Finally a doctor told me I should get
to a more temperate climate as soon as possible,
and this might have been a factor in my being given
a posting back to New Zealand in January 1945.

In between sojourns in hospital and subsequent
medical boards, I did carry out a fair amount of
flying while at Poona. I also received some
marvellous hospitality from a generous Australian
family whose name I have forgotten. I could not
have been a delightful guest because I was badly run
down, felt ill, and had lost a lot of energy. The only
matters of note during my sojourn at Poona are
when I caused a diplomatic protest from the
Portuguese government, also caused my immediate
superior a reprimand, and finally nearly killed
myself while flying on two occasions.

I was sent with a small team to Belgaum to
provide flying tests for a new type of radar, and
while doing these, I was enjoined to stay clear of the
borders of Portuguese Goa. However, I was
required to fly for a minimum time on a certain

course which led directly to the said border, which I inadvertently crossed thereby starting diplomatic activity. It would have been interesting had the Portugese sent up a fighter or two, as I was flying a Spitfire Mk VIII. All I received was a mandatory telling off. Eventually I got fed up with the boredom of training pilots every day, and decided that I should try for an operational posting. At that time I had given up any idea of returning home as the New Zealand authorities had lost touch with us completely, and appeared to have lost any interest in us at all. The RAF were keeping their people overseas for four years or more. My request to return to a squadron was turned down, so I decided that the only way to achieve my desire was to make a nuisance of myself by breaking rules so that they might be pleased to get rid of me.

I took up a Spitfire and proceeded to do aerobatics right over the control tower. I was ordered to go elsewhere, and when I landed Squadron Leader Earnshaw, my closest colleague scoffed at me and said that he could put on a better display. I offered him my Spitfire but he declined and said he would use a Hurricane. This he did, and while doing so, the station commander, a group captain, rang me and demanded the pilot's name. He wished to see Earnshaw, the moment he landed. Poor Earnshaw was duly matted and reprimanded for unbecoming conduct. Nothing was said about my effort. A further foray on my part was prevented by another session in hospital.

On another occasion I was giving a demonstration on alertness to a course of fighter pilots, and managed to 'bounce' them at 25,000 feet. In the mêlée which developed, I got a little too careless in my flying, and my aircraft spun with full throttle applied. It was a most vicious spin with a high rate of rotation. After closing the throttle it took a long time to slow down to a point where the aeroplane recovered from the spin. By this time I was close to the ground in a vertical dive, and I blacked out badly in pulling out. I was totally blind and could not see by how much I was going to clear the ground. I had to keep the G forces applied until I judged the aeroplane was out of its dive and climbing. A bit more G and I could have become unconscious. However, when I thought I was climbing again I put on a little negative G to help a return of blood flow to my head, and when my sight returned I found I was indeed in a gentle climb. I was a little shaken to find how vicious a Spitfire could be if one took liberties with it. A loss of 25,000 feet in a spin was not unusual.

The final little deadly incident took place when I and another pilot were providing air attacks on a practice amphibian landing near Bombay. This was in preparation for a landing near Rangoon. We firstly attacked the landing craft, and I was a bit amused when the gunners on one fired at me while approaching, but abandoned their gun as I went straight at them, by diving to the bottom of their craft. As they did so, the gun barrel elevated and I very nearly hit it. As the landing progressed, we strafed the troops on the beach. A group of officers was obviously enjoying seeing some of their confreres diving prostrate onto the wet sand, so I thought that they should receive some of the same medicine. I came in low off the sea with my propeller no more than feet above the sand and the said officers themselves went flat. It was then that I found that I hadn't enough room to clear a line of jungle trees right in my path. I used emergency boost and hauled the stick back. I could just about hear the branches brushing my underside, but managed to clear the obstacle. That was my last flight on a Spitfire as it turned out, and it was nearly my last activity while alive. That flight was never recorded in my logbook.

We did have some opportunities for relaxation while at Poona. Three of us; Earnshaw, Gandy, and myself, used to go hunting on odd occasions. We didn't have much success, but sometimes had excitement. One such occasion was when we, with our trusty Lee Enfield rifles, travelled away in a landrover and stayed overnight in a dak bungalow. These were small buildings dotted along various routes for the use of sahibs. They were kept clean by the local villagers who were paid for the service. So far as I know we didn't pay anything for their use. The next day we were following a track along the side of a small hill when Gandy suddenly stopped and pointed out a paw mark in a wet patch of the path. "Tiger" he said, "and quite fresh. Can't be more than fifteen minutes old. It's probably in the undergrowth over there at the base of the hill." He pointed out where the tiger should be.

Under his guidance we went back and arranged for beaters to form a line and force the tiger to cross over the top of the hill. Then we climbed to the top of the hill to await the beast. Gandy said, "Peart, you get behind that pile of stones over there", pointing to a small cairn on the edge of the hill.

"And Earnshaw, you get behind that pile over there", pointing to another cairn opposite mine. "I shall wait behind that pile" he said indicating one a little to the rear of ours. The three piles formed a triangle on the top of the hill and the tiger was expected to appear and run straight for Gandy's pile while having to pass between Earnshaw and myself. I had severe doubts that Lee Enfield rifles would stop a tiger let alone kill it. My schoolboy reading on the subject always had hunters with elephant rifles.

There were no handy trees up which I could climb. Also, when I looked across at Earnshaw's pile, it was to see a rifle pointing right at me. If the tiger didn't obligingly run straight between us, and came my way, both Gandy and Earnshaw would be shooting right at me. The tiger would hardly regard me as an obstacle. I didn't like it at all. Bad enough to be attacked by the tiger, but to be shot in the process was too much. I looked around for some fall back position, but there were none. I even had considerable doubts as to my marksmanship. To tell the truth I was in a severe funk.

I could hear the beaters approaching banging tins, shouting, and blowing whistles, so settled down to sell my life dearly. The suspense was terrific until the beaters suddenly appeared out of the undergrowth and no tiger. In relief I climbed to the top of my cairn to see better, and fell over on the loose stones. We went on with our hunt until I found that my leg was hurting so much that I couldn't walk. Upon removing my puttees (worn to stop spear grass from entering the flesh of our legs) and my boot, I found my leg swollen around two puncture wounds. I had been bitten by a snake, probably a krait. Anyway, when I received medical attention, the doctor suggested that while the snake was a big one (judging by the distance between the puncture marks) it must have bitten something shortly before so that I didn't receive the full dose of poison. Also my puttees must have stopped deep penetration of its fangs. I recovered rapidly but my tiger hunt was over. I never had another opportunity. Not that I wanted one.

I duly received my posting back to New Zealand, and was released from hospital to report to a centre in Bombay with a strict injunction that I was to stay quietly in my quarters while there waiting for transport home. If I didn't observe this restriction, I could collapse. I had no opportunity to do any shopping for gifts to take home. I did on one occasion take a gharry into Bombay but didn't stay in town very long. The great day dawned when I was told to get my gear to the docks and board an American troopship by the name of USS *General Mitchell*. Upon boarding, I discovered that I was to share a cabin with quite a number of my fellow countrymen who were also being repatriated. We sailed early the next day, and so my service with the RAF came to an end.

All the time I was in India I had not received my pay, but managed to meet all mess bills and purchases of clothing etc. from two special allowances paid to aircrew serving in the Far East. One was called the Far East allowance, and the other was an operational allowance paid to aircrew on operational service at the front. Both of these were presumably to compensate for the hardships and health and other risks associated with such service. While I found that some of the fighting was harder in the Middle East for example, nothing I had encountered elsewhere could compare with the terrible flying conditions, the severe climate, and the diseases to which servicemen were exposed. Indeed, statistics published later alleged that annual casualties in the British 14th Army amounted to half a million per year from disease alone. A few of us were awarded a DFC, and this meant a lot to us, as decorations were very sparingly awarded in the Far East, unlike in other theatres. I left with an unfortunate dislike of Hindus, but an admiration for many of the Indian tribes, especially the Ghurkhas, and the hill tribes around Imphal. The Nagas, Karens, Kachins, and Chins come particularly to mind.

Even aboard the ship we didn't manage to escape the last vestiges of India. Perhaps because of the conditioning of my own experiences, plus what I had observed affecting others, I didn't have much affection for the country. I had suffered dysentery (and still had it), dengue fever, jungle sores, prickly heat, and a general rundown in my health, partly through poor food, but also due to the wealth of disease organisms that seemed to infest the ground, the air, and the water. Fortunately the quota given to me was nothing compared with what others suffered, and died from. Malaria was rife (I missed that in India), amoebic dysentery also caught many (I fortunately only had bacterial dysentery which was bad enough). Therefore ingrained in my mind was a perception of everything in India crawling with bugs and bacteria and disease.

Many villages had no provision for waste, and the populace just excreted in an area of open ground in a ring around the village. One had to keep to the entrance tracks to avoid walking through it all. Villages were full of pi-dogs which had to feed on something. In cities such as Calcutta and Bombay the sahibs (which is what all whites were called) were open game for stealing, pilfering and cheating in one way or another. One exception applied to our personal bearers (servants) whose employment depended on their honesty. In Assam I was well served, but didn't own very much to be relieved of anyway. But one bearer I had in Poona, a Mohammedan by name of Kulu Khan, was scrupulously honest, and I would have trusted him with anything. He was a real professional and we got along famously. He told me once that I was very careless, and required his full attention. A very fine person with three wives and quite a number of children. He was always asking for time off because one of his wives was having a baby.

While waiting in a holding depot for our ship home, I shared a room with a provost officer (military police) and two days before we left, he to Britain and myself to New Zealand, he had his wallet stolen while we were asleep. The thieves had entered our room, explored all the usual hiding places for valuables including inside the pillowcases under one's sleeping head, and had taken his wallet from just that place. I, with my usual carelessness had left my wallet in my trouser pocket at the head of my bed. The thieves hadn't thought anyone would have been so stupid and had missed it. There was an awful fuss and the provost officer gave all the Indian staff twenty-four hours to return his wallet or else dire things would happen. The wallet was returned intact within the twenty-four hours, much to my surprise.

There wasn't much love of the British Raj in India at that time, and a sahib caught on his own by an Indian crowd could expect some violence. One day, all the others had gone into Bombay to purchase presents, while I, under medical instructions was prevented. However, I had to take something home so I decided to make a quick trip in. I hired a gharry which deposited me in a bazaar of some sort where I bought some sari edging of gold embroidery. (I think it was real gold because it hasn't tarnished in all these years.) When I wished to return home no taxis, gharries, or any form of transport was available. I asked some stall keepers to order me a taxi, (with the usual baksheesh of course) and while I waited I became the target of unwanted attention from a growing crowd.

A taxi did turn up, and I got in, but the driver refused to move until I paid him an exorbitant fee. The crowd started looking nasty to me, and I thought it wise to get out of there quickly. The driver refused to budge so I drew my revolver and put the muzzle to his ear telling him if he didn't get moving immediately, I would shoot him and drive myself. I think that I meant it too, because some of the crowd looked as though they might attack. Anyway the driver got moving and we returned to our barracks. I paid him the going rate for a taxi, against his vociferous protests, and that was that. I have often thought since whether or not I would have pulled the trigger, and I am sure that I would have done so if I believed that my life was in danger. The driver was convinced.

20
Return to New Zealand

Upon leaving Bombay aboard the ship USS *General Mitchell*, I broached a bottle of Grants whisky that I had been saving for just such an occasion. Six of us had assembled in our cabin, and intended to settle the whole bottle in one go as a celebration. Glasses were laid out, and I ceremoniously removed the cap. Each chap present received a generous portion. Some couldn't wait until I had finished before taking a sip. Nothing was said and I had my first long awaited taste. It had no taste, and could have been coloured water, weak tea, or another unmentionable liquid. The thieving Indians had had the last laugh. Upon close inspection it was found that the bottle had a hole drilled in its base. This had been cunningly stopped up again after the whisky had been drained off and a liquid of like colour substituted. The thieves were nothing if not ingenious, but it helped to set in concrete my dislike of Hindus and India.

The ship was an American naval vessel, equipped for troop carrying, and the on board rules were somewhat restrictive. Most desirable deck spots were out of bounds, and not all of us could fit into the available open air places at one time. There were only two meals each day, but these were substantial, and attractively prepared. The weather was fine and calm, and we made good progress to our first port of call, Melbourne. There were two troop holds, and these held Italian prisoners of war. Each hold had three levels crammed with Italian servicemen.

I was placed in command of one hold and my task was to inspect the hold each day accompanied by two armed American GIs. I went unarmed because I could see no reason to have a revolver which would really be useless in the event of an attack anyway, and the prisoners couldn't do much with two rifles if they did overpower the guards. I was proved right because there was no attempt at attack, but I was pelted with small cardboard swastikas which did me no harm. I just grinned at the Italian fascists. On several occasions abandon ship drills were rehearsed, and it was my responsibility to see that the prisoners of war were brought out of the hold to get clear of the ship before it sank. It did cross my mind that I might have to give up any idea of getting clear myself. Fortunately the real test did not eventuate.

We crossed the Indian Ocean in calm seas and arrived at Melbourne where the prisoners of war were disembarked. We had no opportunity of going ashore as the ship left for New Zealand within a few hours. The crossing of the notorious Tasman Sea was calm and early on a Sunday morning we entered the Auckland harbour to hear over the ship's broadcast system Uncle Tom's children's choir. It brought back memories of my years as a child and a young man before I went overseas. It seemed so long ago. I looked around at the green hills, the homes on the slopes, and other remembered landmarks, and felt an enormous sense of relief. I was home, alive and safe, if not in very good health.

Upon disembarking from the USS *General Mitchell* we were duly sprayed, dusted down with DDT, and processed at a unit situated somewhere clear of the wharves. Most were given immediate rail passes and bookings to their home destinations. The whole process seemed to be aimed at getting us home as soon as possible, and was most efficiently conducted. However, in my case I was given a medical examination and was detained for a series of tests. I seem to remember that this took some days, but I wasn't feeling terribly motivated to do anything but relax and feel pleased to be home in New Zealand again.

Eventually I was given a medical grading '3', which was totally unfit for further service, so I was told. I also received a rail pass to Hamilton. I had a number of flimsy suitcases which were sent ahead in the guard's van. My uniform was unfortunately very worn and faded. On arrival at Hamilton I went to some friends of the family, a Mr and Mrs Russell, where I stayed the night awaiting the bus to my home town, Raglan the next day.

Two incidents occurred which worried me greatly at the time. The first happened on the Frankton railway station from where I had to take a taxi to Hamilton. I had to traverse a long length of platform and cross an overhead bridge to reach the taxi rank. I had one of my flimsy suitcases (Indian made) with me, and when I lifted it onto the platform the handle came off. I then hoisted it on to my shoulder, and it fell apart scattering clothing and other effects onto the platform. Some people passing thought this very funny and laughed most audibly at my discomfiture. No one saw any need to offer assistance. A policeman fortunately came along and ordered everyone away in short order. He helped me to collect my belongings together and to stuff them into the remains of my suitcase. I weighed only just over eight stone, and I was feeling rather weak and shaky at the time. He kindly helped me to the taxi stand and hired a taxi for me. I felt quite churned up about the whole business which didn't say much for my first contact with the New Zealand public.

The second incident occurred the same evening at dusk, when I was riding a borrowed bicycle along the street to the Russell's with another suitcase I had collected from the Hamilton railway station. The street inclined uphill and I had to dismount, but in doing so, my case caught the handlebars, causing me to veer towards the footpath. A young woman who was walking down the footpath opposite, screamed loudly and ran off down the street. Then three young men appeared and ran up to me very aggressively. We had words. They finally went on their way with threats and warnings, leaving me very disturbed and convinced that something must be very wrong. Later it turned out that, unbeknown to me, attacks had been made for some time on a number of young women in the vicinity by a person on a bicycle, and someone in air force uniform was suspected. Indeed an airman was arrested later, and it transpired that he was a mental case. These two events shook me.

The next day I caught the bus to Raglan, and found a small crowd awaiting its arrival. There was my mother and young brother John from the family. We had a fond greeting, and by then the crowd had melted away, so I didn't have an opportunity to talk to any of the people I knew. Apparently I didn't look the smartly dressed air force officer they had expected. Later I gleaned that I looked more like a scarecrow. The usual kindly formal welcome home ceremonies followed, and my family did their utmost to let me have as peaceful a time as possible. My biggest concern was that I couldn't digest the rich food. A beautiful roast dinner which had been the subject of much dreaming while I was away, and which my mother had specially prepared, made me ill. Also I had a few habits which upset my mother.

What with dysentery, flies, and foreign objects found in our food in Africa and India, I had always pulled my food apart for close inspection before eating it, and this habit was so ingrained that it had become an automatic reaction whenever I ate. That took quite a while to eradicate. A second problem concerned fevers, which came and went at regular intervals, and attacks of diarrhoea which plagued me. However, apart from those problems, I was quite healthy, although much under-weight. I found out much later that my family were very worried about my psychological condition. I must admit that I took about three years to re-accustom myself to normal society.

I was given a three-month rail pass for myself and two others, as part of my repatriation leave. My mother, John and myself had a wonderful tour of the South Island, meeting relatives and seeing the sights. Using the same pass, I later visited my twin brother, Roger, at Taieri EFTS, where he was a flying instructor, and found out how undisciplined my flying had become. I had learned a lot of bad habits while away. He and I had a wonderful time socially, and everyone was very kind, but I found it hard to fall back into the usual social regimes, and hard to meet the expectations of partners at dances etc. Indeed I felt that I needed to learn how to relate to other people all over again, and this worried me more than a little.

My repatriation leave finally finished, and I reported for duty at RNZAF Headquarters, Wellington. There I was interviewed by a Wing Commander Newton who told me I was being posted to a squadron in the Pacific Islands for further operational duty. This came as quite a shock as I had hoped for a spell away from combat, and in any case my health was not yet restored. I explained that I wasn't yet fit, but could probably help for a while passing on all that I had learnt from the RAF Central Gunnery School. He bluntly told me that the RAF pilots returning still had something to learn, and that we weren't much use to the RNZAF until we had assimilated how things were done up in the Islands. He said that I would do as I was ordered and go to the Pacific. However, when I mentioned that I would first require a medical clearance (remembering that I was classified grade 3), he said that would not be necessary. I left his office on a note of firm disagreement. He must have discussed our meeting with others, because back at my accommodation I had a telephone call from a Squadron Leader Harvey asking if I was interested in doing an instructor's course at the Central Flying School. I said yes, and was then posted to CFS, Woodbourne where flying instructor training was carried out.

21

Instructor Training at Woodbourne

We were a small group made up mainly of ex-RAF pilots who no doubt had fallen foul of the same attitude that I had encountered. We started our training on Tiger Moths and enjoyed all the gracious living presented by the standard officers' mess, a terrific contrast to the conditions we had borne for years. We had a whole book of teaching instructions to learn by heart and then to say, word perfect, while flying. Also one had to be able to demonstrate each flying manoeuvre perfectly, including aerobatics. Thus firstly we had to practise flying until we were perfect, and then we had to fly perfectly while telling a pupil (usually another course member) just what we were doing. When adroitness at doing this had been mastered, we transferred to Harvards and did the same again. I enjoyed this greatly, once I had dropped my operational flying habits which were frowned upon.

The Harvard was a nice machine to fly, not like the ones we used in India, which were hard to land without ground looping. The course ended with a test by the chief flying instructor, which included a forced landing, just as taught to a pupil. In my case, I was doing perfectly when the wind direction changed forcing me to abandon part of my patter (the teaching talk was called patter), and to complete the actual forced landing. The CFI did not ask me to do another, but signified that he was satisfied. I passed out as 'proficient' to be an instructor, and would, under normal circumstances have been posted to a training unit instructing on Harvards. However, the war ended, and after a short period we were interviewed to ascertain what we wished to do in the future.

The end of the Second World War occurred when I was second pilot of a Hudson bomber on a trip to the North Island. Strangely enough my brother Roger was a passenger with us when we took off from Paraparaumu on our return to Woodbourne. The captain was Squadron Leader Cunningham, and on take-off he must have had some problem on his mind for he let the throttles slip back so badly that it looked as though we were going to hit the nearby hills. When I drew his attention to the problem and frantically started to tighten my seat belt ready for the crash, he thrust the throttles through the gate and we just made it over the top of the hill. On our way across Cook Strait we were told that the war had ended. We landed at Woodbourne to find everyone celebrating, and possibly we were the last aeroplane airborne in New Zealand at the end of the war.

My own reaction was muted. I just felt suddenly relaxed. I thought to myself "I have made it. I am alive. I have survived." Dancing, drinking, and cavorting around as others were doing, just didn't seem to me to fit the situation. I thought about all the chaps who had been killed, and about my own very narrow escapes, and just wanted to be alone. I had behind me over two years of operational activity without any but very short rests, somewhere between sixty and seventy individual combats with enemy aircraft, hundreds of sorties involving strafing of enemy positions and facilities, and many episodes of being bombed and strafed, as well as surviving shocking flying and living conditions at various times. I think my poem, *The Scramble*, might explain my feelings best.

Up Up Up! We claw for height
The ground below sinks from our sight.
Noses high our Spitfires soar
Turn port, turn port says Control
Bandits below, five or more!

Our sleek craft race through the burning blue
We look for the foe just we few
Tally Ho! They're down below.
Black specks menacing look
The bandits, they're Focke-Wulf 190s.

Whirling planes, peril dire.
Who is it there all afire?
Guns are flashing as the fight proceeds
More go down to meet their Maker
The land below their remains receives.

Some Mother's son is lost
His country to protect.
Some remain to count the cost

And wonder what fate has to offer next
Another day have they to reflect.

The fight is over, the survivors dive
Earthward bound a haven seeking
Relief in their hearts to be alive.
Owe they thanks for their safe keeping?
Surely to our Lord is that honour due.

Home sweet home, the war is over.
Relief from fear, from dread, from death.
Memories of dark clouds and air clear blue,
Of old pals and high flight, furious jousts
in the sky.
Homage to all fighter pilots is their due.
Knights of the Air!

A silent tear crawls down my cheek. I really do owe
the Lord my God.

When I started at the CFS I wore a flight
lieutenant's rank insignia, but it was brought to my
attention that in the RNZAF I was only a pilot
officer, and I was to wear that rank forthwith. I had
forgotten that I had been promoted acting-flight
lieutenant by the RAF. This reduction in rank made
me the most junior officer on the station, with
officers who had joined years later much senior to
me. While I suppose it was a strictly accurate
interpretation of the administrative situation at that
time, it was badly handled and I felt insulted. I
retaliated by submitting a claim for pay which had
been overlooked over the whole period I was in
India. This was ignored, and I consulted a solicitor
who forced the RNZAF to pay a sum of about

£700, which was quite an amount in those days. The restoration of my rank as flight lieutenant was made shortly after, so it appeared that I had won that battle.

When we were interviewed regarding our future, I indicated that I wished to be demobilised and couldn't help noticing the signs of relief on the faces of the interviewing officers as one after another we chose to go back to civilian life. Within a short time we were released from a unit situated in Wellington for that purpose, and I started to wear civilian clothes again, a rather strange experience. I was placed on the officer's reserve list, and later was given some free flying with the local aero club to keep my hand in. However, except for a short attachment to a headquarters unit in the RNZAF years later, that finished my association with the RNZAF. I was twenty-three years old.

Epilogue

After being de-mobbed from the air force, the future became a major consideration. I had been granted my long awaited engineering cadetship with the New Zealand Government Public Works Department and this opened the way to my achieving a career in civil engineering. This required an academic qualification involving a minimum of four years university study. My physical health was not particularly good at the time. I was under weight at about nine stone, still recovering from recurring problems with dysentery and fevers arising I believe from previous attacks of malaria and dengue. I still had difficulty in adjusting to the diet at home. Regularly each month a bout of fever returned, causing me to feel rather unwell. It was also quite hard to keep warm in the temperate climate of the Waikato. Civilian clothes felt rather strange.

Even more worryingly I seemed to find it hard to fit into a civilian way of life, to play a normal part in day to day social interactions. I was absorbed with watching my back and felt uncomfortable with having anyone out of sight behind me. This might have been partly the result of sojourns in enemy countries when the potential for clandestine attack upon one's person was present for much of the time. It took me a long time to adjust to the safer environment of my home country.

I am sure that many other ex-servicemen suffered the same problems to a greater or lesser degree. One just had to adjust and try to be sensitive to the requirements of modern civilian life as quickly as possible. Medical advice on the fever problem was later received from a doctor who had been trained at a school for tropical medicine. He told me that, provided I didn't stay in tropical countries in the future, my fevers would die away in a few years. This advice proved correct. All in all, it took about three years to become fully re-assimilated into normal society.

Beginning university study after six years absence from school proved most challenging. Subjects had advanced and expanded. I found that my past schooling in mathematics and science was deficient in both scope and range. This deficiency had to be overcome in the course of the first year's study, to compete later with the younger students who were a year or two ahead of us in the academic stakes. Other ex-servicemen were in a similar position. In general most of us weathered the first demanding years at the expense of long study hours and very, very hard work. Towards the end, having caught up, our studies became enjoyable and we managed to take part in the university social life. I graduated with an engineering degree from the University of New Zealand in 1949 in the minimum possible time. Then followed years of practical experience in construction and design with the Ministry of Works as it was then called, followed by periods in a management role and a lengthy period in the planning field in its narrowest and widest sense. I finally ended my career in the interesting position of District Commissioner of Works, Wellington.

I feel fortunate that as the years have passed, I have enjoyed remarkably good health. I have also been fortunate in pursuing my civil engineering career during the heyday of the modern development of New Zealand, when the design and construction of hydro-electric schemes, airports, motorways, and other works were essential to New Zealand's future. Planning in resource, urban and rural development, and environmental fields also absorbed much of my later career. I finished with an administrative and advisory role in most of the above activities.

I have now had the pleasure of having been retired for the last twenty-five years with a very supportive wife, three adult children, and seven grandchildren. I thank the Lord for an exciting and very fulfilling life.

Appendix A
Aerial Marksmanship

In later years I visited my close friend and colleague Larry Cronin in Australia. He and I had joined 81 Squadron together in 1942 and had left at the same time in 1944. During a conversation he wryly remarked: "If we had been anything like decent shots we could have become high scoring aces ourselves." He was quite right because we both had been in enough combat situations to warrant the comment. However, in spite of his observation both of us had benefited from the law of averages, which in this instance implies that if you shoot at a target enough times you are bound to hit it sooner or later. So, both he and I ran up decent scores. However, I found myself time and again frustrated by missing when in a position to shoot my opponent down. I cannot recall reading any books written by fighter pilots of World War II where a detailed analysis has been made of aerial marksmanship and the tactics used in combat, nor about the difficulties which were encountered. In retrospect it might now be useful to comment on some of these problems.

I have commented on the need to have very sharp eyesight and the ability to change the focus of one's vision at will over a range of distances from infinity to near proximity. Failure to achieve this put one at a disadvantage in that an opponent could well have seen you before you have detected him, and he becomes the attacker rather than the defender. All fighters were then quite small in size, and could be seen as just specks in the sky at a distance of about three miles. When it is appreciated that the turning radius of a Spitfire was also about three miles it explains why so many pilots in combat found an empty sky after a turn. Conversely they could also find themselves suddenly in the middle of a mêlée after flying in what they thought was a clear sky. So one had to be very alert at all times and scan the sky all around, particularly the area around the sun.

General all-round vision was achieved by constant weaving while the regular cocking of a wing to cover the sun allowed coverage of that area. One never ever flew a straight line for that could be fatal. One also had to develop a sixth sense of recognition, for it didn't pay to mistake a group of the enemy for one of ours. When seen as specks a sense of shape and formation type came into play and strangely very few mistakes were made. If radar was available and a controller was in charge this of course helped greatly, but outside Britain there were many occasions when we didn't have such a service.

Speeds were approximately three to four times those of the First World War fighters and the aeroplanes were also much more powerful and heavy. A Spitfire weighed something in excess of three tons, fully fuelled and armed. With head-on closing speeds in the region of more than eight hundred miles per hour it could be a matter of seconds after early detection that your opponent was upon you. It was therefore wise to be wide-awake at all times and to have considered your defence tactics beforehand. Usually this was the responsibility of the leader of the group, be it a pair or a full squadron. In spite of all care, pilots did have their off days when they could be caught napping, and this was frequently when they were shot down. Very often no-one would see them go. They just disappeared in the heat of battle. It was quite rare to see them bale out and few from our squadron ever made their way back.

In actual combat the fighter pilot had to be careful to avoid losing control because of stalling in a high-speed turn for instance, or blacking out badly under the effects of high gravity. Such was the power of a fighter that at full throttle a loss of control usually meant violent gyrations, and some time to recover, not to mention a considerable loss of valuable height. One's opponent also had an advantage in that your manoeuvres became predictable and one became an easier target. While the Spitfire was a most tolerant machine in all sorts of situations it could be vicious if mishandled and I suspect that some pilots paid the price for this.

The armament of a Spitfire during most of the war comprised two 20 mm cannon with high explosive, incendiary, and armour piercing rounds alternating, and four Browning 0.303 inch machine guns with a high rate of fire. These were located in the wings approximately five or six feet below the pilot's line of sight and of course well out to either side. All were carefully aligned and harmonised to provide a dense pattern of fire at 200 yards and again at 600 yards when the missiles fell back again through the line of sight. If one's opponent was hit by the full weight of this fire serious damage would ensue and the target could disintegrate or explode with severe consequences for the pilot or crew. This is what every fighter pilot aimed to achieve when he fired his guns. Because of this placing of the guns in relation to the line of sight however, it was most important to judge range correctly before opening fire. On several occasions I missed entirely because I was too close and sometimes I suspect my attackers had the same problem. Anyway they missed.

The enemy had armament similar to ours, except for the Italian Macchi 202s, which were only lightly armed. Both the Spitfire and German fighters had armour protecting the pilot's back and legs, while the Japanese didn't have this, so we were told. However it now appears from some translations of Japanese pilots' memoirs that at least some fighters did have armour. Notably the Oscars against which we were pitched in India and Burma.

Now we come to the vexed question of poor marksmanship. To my mind this could be placed in two categories. Firstly there was what was called snap shooting where a pilot whipped his aeroplane into what he sensed was the correct firing position, almost without any attempt at aiming, and fired. Some of the top aces had this ability but the great majority of fighter pilots lacked it completely, and I must have been one of these. Secondly there was the aimed shot where the pilot used his fighter as a gun platform and made allowance for range and deflection. This was much more difficult than it sounds.

A whole range of variables interfered with the achievement of a successful aimed shot. To begin with one must conquer the big rush of adrenalin and the degree of high excitement which interferes with calculation. Indeed in my early combats I think I forgot to use my reflector sight, so close was the target, and such was my excitement. Of course I missed and the enemy escaped to fight another day. Then there was the all-important matter of flying accurately, an essential ingredient to using the aircraft as a gun platform. This was far from easy when carrying out an attacking manoeuvre while keeping an eye on one's own tail and facing return fire during an attack, especially in the case where the target was a bomber or a defended ground position.

In attacking bombers or defended ground targets I always used slipping and skidding to mislead the opposing gunners during my approach and straightened out just before firing. The same applied during the breakaway. Time was very short to switch from unstable to stable flight and this was a skill acquired only with practice. Being quite a large target a bomber was much easier to hit than a fighter. Range was an all-important ingredient and many pilots tended to open fire out of range. Range was difficult to judge and a special adjustable grid was part of the reflector sight but I believe it was rarely used because one had to adjust to the dimensions of the enemy machine beforehand and there just wasn't time to do this while entering combat.

If the attack was made at squadron or flight strength the leader of the formation usually had the first shot which could be a calculated one. By that time the enemy was alerted and taking evasive action so those following usually had to do snap shooting during the ensuing combat. Much depended on the tactics of the enemy. In the case of German opponents we aimed to get on their tail and stay there because of the Spitfire's superior manoeuvrability. The Germans generally attacked and dived away. The situation was reversed against the Japanese because the manoeuvrability of their fighters was legendary.

Finally the whole business of aerial fighting became much more difficult when one was up against superior opponents, a situation which did pertain from time to time during the Second World War. This applied over France when the Focke-Wulf 190 made its first appearance in 1942 I think, when the RAF had mostly Mk V Spitfires, and again later in the early stages of the North African campaign in 1942 after the Torch landings in Morocco and Algeria when we flew tropicalised Mk V Spitfires against FW 190s and ME 109Gs.

To my mind the whole business of aerial fighting was like trying to shoot accurately from a slippery moving surface at a target gyrating like a blowfly. Some could do it successfully, but most couldn't. It must be remembered though, that the great majority of combats consisted of an initial clash possibly followed by a short fight lasting a few minutes only. They were quite deadly as many inexperienced pilots can attest to. Much of what I have said applies to dogfighting in much longer combats when the odds were not always even, such as one pilot flying on his own against many. This did happen to me on two occasions when I felt what skills I had were rather stretched. It has happened to others too!

Towards the end of my career I attended a course in aerial combat and marksmanship in India where some, but not all, of the above described problems were dealt with. The course made evident to me the inadequacy of gunnery training given before we reached our operational squadrons in Britain. Having completed this specialised schooling in India I was very keen to try out what I had learnt but it was not to be. By this time the Allied air force had achieved command of the air over the enemy and opportunities for aerial combat had become very limited. As a result squadron activities were concentrated mainly on ground attack, which of course also demanded the use of some of the skills outlined above.

I have not expanded on other facets of aerial fighting such as weather, lack of navigational and night landing devices, gun stoppages, physical demands on the body, and mental and physical health. These do not really come under the category of memoirs but they are touched upon in the body of the journal. The last attribute, which I believe the fighter pilot must have, is an ingrained sense of survival. Its absence when faced with seemingly impossible outcomes I am sure has cost many lives.

This completes my commentary on the problems besetting fighter pilots when carrying out their duties and I hope that the reader now has some appreciation of the difficulties faced by a combat pilot in the Second World War. Perhaps in RAF terms I can be accused of 'shooting a line' but what the hell!

Appendix B

DFC Citation and Combat Victories

A Distinguished Flying Cross was awarded to Alan McGregor Peart on 2nd June 1944 while he was with 81 Squadron. The DFC citation reads:

> "Flying Officer Peart is a keen and courageous fighter who has destroyed five enemy aircraft and damaged several more. He has taken part in a very large number of sorties and set a fine example of devotion to duty throughout."

Aces High by Christopher Shores, published by Grub Street in 1994, credits Alan Peart with six combat victories, plus one shared destroyed and nine damaged. Interestingly Alan achieved combat victories against the Italians, Germans and the Japanese, most but not all of which he has described in this book. He was determined to describe only those for which his memory remained clear. His full list of combat successes are recorded as follows:

Date	Enemy Aircraft	Type flown	Serial No.	Rego	Location
1 Dec 1942	S-84	Spitfire V		FL-D	Bône harbour
1 Dec 1942	S-84 Damaged	Spitfire V		FL-D	Bône harbour
31 Dec 1942	ME109 Damaged			PH	Bône area
23 Apr 1943	ME109G Damaged	Spitfire IX	EN207	FL-D	Beja
25 Apr 1943	ME109	Spitfire IX	EN204	FL-E	Medjez-el-Bab
16 Jul 1943	ME109G Damaged	Spitfire Vc	EN207	FL-4	Catania
28 Aug 1943	ME109	Spitfire IX	EN513	FL-J	Sicily
13 Sep 1943	Do217 ($^1/_3$)	Spitfire IX		FL-B	Salerno
13 Feb 1944	Oscars Damaged (2)	Spitfire VIII		FL-D	Burma front
16 Mar 1944	Oscar	Spitfire VIII		FL-B	Near Paunybyin
17 Mar 1944	Oscar	Spitfire VIII		FL-E	Broadway
17 Apr 1944	Oscar	Spitfire VIII		FL-D	Palel
17 Apr 1944	Oscars Damaged (2)	Spitfire VIII		FL-D	Palel
14 May 1944	Oscar Damaged	Spitfire VIII		FL-D	Imphal Valley

Index

216